# HOLY COOPERATION!

## BUILDING GRACEFUL ECONOMIES

ANDREW McLEOD

CASCADE *Books* · Eugene, Oregon

HOLY COOPERATION!
Building Graceful Economies

Cascade Books
A Division of Wipf and Stock Publishers
199 W. 8th Ave., Suite 3
Eugene, OR 97401

www.wipfandstock.com

ISBN 13: 978-1-55635-635-3

*Cataloging-in-Publication data:*

McLeod, Andrew.

    Holy cooperation! : building graceful economies / Andrew McLeod.

    xvi + 124 p. ; 23 cm.

    Includes bibliographical references.

    ISBN 13: 978-1-55635-244-7 (alk. paper)

    1. Cooperation. 2. Economics—Religious aspects—Christianity. I. Sine, Tom. II. Author.

BR115.E3 M335 2009

Manufactured in the U.S.A.

# contents

# *foreword*

Frankly, this book couldn't be timelier. All readers are aware of rising food and gas prices and the volatility of the global economy as this book is launched. What isn't yet evident to most readers is the growing vulnerability of not just the poor and the working poor in North America but increasingly the middle class as well. Andrew McLeod has discovered some very important linkages between vital faith and creating cooperatives that have the potential to give our communities a more sustainable way of life.

One of the most pro-active ways that churches and community service organizations can respond to this emerging crisis is to give birth to a range of cooperative enterprises. These cooperatives have the potential to enable people in our local communities to create local and sustainable ways to produce much more of their own food. But they also have the possibility to create cooperative economic initiatives and even forms of social entrepreneurship that can enable communities to sustain life for us and our most vulnerable neighbors in increasingly uncertain times.

The challenge after you read this book will be to persuade your church to shift from the soup kitchen mentality to becoming a birthing center for cooperative enterprises that empower those who are struggling. You might suggest the daring idea of having your church start a small agricultural cooperative by offering your church lawn as the first resource to get the ball rolling. You may find a few daring souls who are ready to explore creating housing cooperatives like those which are beginning to emerge all over the country, to both reduce costs and create more sustainable mutual care communities.

Many who read this book and become convinced by Andrew's arguments that biblical faith calls us beyond individualistic lifestyles to a more cooperative way of life will find many in their churches are not ready to be convinced. But I would be surprised if you couldn't find other followers of Jesus in your community, plus those of other faiths and non-religious motivations, who are ready to join you in making a beginning.

Andrew will, in the coming pages, take you on a very important journey. Be open to new ideas and be sure to make notes as you read of ways you might be able to launch small cooperatives in your community that make possible a more sustainable future for you and your neighbors in these troubled times.

Tom Sine
Author of *The New Conspirators:*
*Creating the Future One Mustard Seed at a Time*
www.thenewconspirators.com

# gratitude

I would never have completed this work on my own, so I must acknowledge the contributions of everyone who helped make this work possible. There are too many for me to name, but please know that I am deeply grateful for your support, feedback, and encouragement. Of course, a few people deserve special recognition.

I am deeply grateful to everyone who has been involved in the projects that are described in this book. Without your vision, courage, and hard work, I wouldn't have had much to write here. I wish that there had been time to talk to you as part of the research for this work, and pray that our paths cross soon.

Thanks to Jim Shulruff for telling me that God likes co-ops, and for reminding me of John the Baptist at exactly the right moment. Thanks to Mendy Lugar for giving up your Bible when called to do so. Thanks also to Stephanie Richards for giving me the other book I needed.

Thank you Jonathan Wilson-Hartgrove for editing the paper that was the seed for this book, for telling me that it was only the beginning of something much bigger, and for editing that once I wrote it.

I must thank my parents, Don and Susan, and my sister, Elizabeth, for your detailed editing, support, patience, and help with my technical difficulties during my final "writer's holiday."

I am grateful to many friends and church mates who read and commented on all the writings which have built towards this book. There are too many of you to name, but I have to single out Ben Dryfoos-Guss and Phil Owen for especially thoughtful and detailed feedback; and Sister Laura Swan for some excellent research leads.

I also want to thank my many colleagues and friends who have helped me grasp the transformative potential of cooperatives and have that carry on in the same direction found in the book of Acts. These have taken many forms, which will be briefly addressed in a way that should provide a basic understanding and avenues for further exploration.

These chapters will show both the ways that the church has engaged the subject of economics, and the ways that Christians have organized outside of the church. This history will show that the ideas in this book may be unfamiliar, but they are older than the Bible and collectively make up a continual thread by which people have tried to live by Jesus's teachings.

Chapter 5 will examine the monastic movement that began in the third century, during the time that Christianity was becoming a single established religion under the Roman Empire. This chapter will look at the dramatic transformation from a decentralized network of small egalitarian gatherings into the Roman Catholic Church, which is now one of the world's oldest and largest organizations.

Chapter 6 addresses the lay religious communities that proliferated from medieval to modern times, both within the official church and in response to its worldly power. This chapter will also address secular communism and how it relates to Christian attempts to establish a just social order, including the liberation theology movement.

Chapter 7 will examine modern faith-based cooperation in a way that provides a framework to help understand the ways that it might be applied. In this section, I have chosen to focus on organizations that can be easily researched on the Internet. They may not be the best examples of what is possible, but they will be available to the casual researcher who wishes to learn more. I have only presented a brief glance at a small number of examples; a book could be written about each of these.

## COOPERATION FOR TODAY

The final section addresses our current situation. It will show that the cooperation described in the Bible is not an outdated way of acting out the teachings of Jesus and may provide us with some essential clues about how to create a more peaceful and just world.

Chapter 8 addresses the established principles of the world's cooperative movement, and examines similarities and differences with Christian values and practices. Christianity and cooperatives have much in common, but they are not identical, and any attempt to bridge those differences should not gloss them over.

The final chapter provides a detailed look at the problems facing us today, and how specific models might be expanded and combined to address some of our more challenging economic and social problems.

The conclusion will provide suggestions about how to apply the cooperative model. I hope that readers come away with a clear idea of how to apply cooperation, and not just why.

## EXPLAINING MYSELF

I am not a biblical scholar in any official sense. I write from a background that is primarily rooted in the study and practice of cooperatives, which is a generally secular affair. I hope to show how Christians might approach cooperation, and why they might benefit from more cooperative forms of organizing.

I use the *New Living Translation* of the Bible. From what I know of the various translations, this provides a healthy level of engagement with the original source texts in Greek and Hebrew. Mostly I use that translation because it was given to me as part of a series of events that set me on the road to this writing.

This book is the result of much study and personal exploration, but it cannot fully capture the complexity of the subject at hand. So I shall content myself with trying to provide a lay perspective on some avenues for further investigation. I believe that every writer is biased, and that a reader is best served by an understanding of that bias. For that reason, I offer a brief history of my own relationship with Jesus.

I grew up in a vaguely Protestant household. My family sometimes attended Methodist and Presbyterian churches without giving me the idea that either denomination reflected some exclusive truth. I didn't even know the difference between Methodists and Presbyterians. Even so, I became quite interested in Christianity during high school, and was fortunate enough to be guided by a couple youth pastors who encouraged my tendency to ask questions.

My faith deepened, and I went so far as to offer my life to Christ as a teenager (with anticlimactic results). However, I gradually learned that many Christians were not so interested in my questions. In college I lost interest in religion, except for viewing it as an obstacle to liberation.

After college I became one of nearly thirty co-owners of the New Riverside Café, a democratically managed vegetarian restaurant. This institution of the Minnesota counterculture was founded in the 1970s under the guidance of a Catholic priest, Father William Teska. At the time, I never wondered why a representative of one of the world's great hierarchies might have created a nonhierarchical organization.

Over the next decade, I developed a passion for cooperatives that had a distinctly spiritual element. For many years, I did not see it as being tied to a specific faith. It gradually began to dawn on me that Christian teachings were essentially supportive of what I was doing.

A few years ago, I found myself in a small cave in New Mexico with a friend who was training to be a rabbi. We had an encounter with some vacationing Israelis, which cast an entirely new light on my work and led to my creating a Web site about Christian cooperation.[1]

For the past two years, I have been attending primarily evangelical churches, and I am struck by the blossoming interest in community building, both in that movement and in many other churches that I have visited. I am excited and inspired by what I see happening with the followers of Jesus, and am proud to count myself among them.

I have done my best to faithfully reflect what the Bible teaches, and to accurately describe the activities of Christian cooperators throughout history. I hope that any errors I may have made will not distract readers from appreciating the overall message, which is sound and obvious enough that I feel confident addressing it without formal theological training.

I know that this book is only the beginning of such a study, and it should not be taken as the last word on anything. I hope that you find it enjoyable and challenging, and that this is the start of a conversation that inspires and encourages you in your own search for a more cooperative life. Thank you for reading.

---

1. This Web site may be found at http://www.bookofacts.info.

*one*

# HOLY COOPERATION

## THE BIBLICAL WAY OF ORGANIZATION

The biblical book called Acts serves as the most comprehensive record of Christianity's origins, which includes a prominent story of democratic and voluntary sharing of resources. The believers avoided concentration of power in a way that provides us with a very challenging example. Even if we set aside the miraculous aspects of the account, we see a social transformation that is its own kind of miracle.

Put yourself in the shoes of the first Christians and try to imagine what it would have been like to participate in the events recorded in the first part of the book of Acts. If you have a Bible handy, you might want to take this opportunity to read the first six chapters of Acts.

Jesus had raised the hopes of his followers that the long-awaited Messiah had arrived, but his gruesome execution cast doubt on that notion. Several days after his death, Jesus was suddenly back. He showed himself to believers in a variety of settings for more than a month, then abruptly rose into the sky and was gone. It must have been a very strange time. People were certainly struggling to make sense of it all and were surely disappointed by this second departure.

Just over a week later, many of Jesus's followers had gathered for a Jewish festival of the first harvest, called Shavuot. It turned out to be quite an event, which is now marked by the holiday of Pentecost. The miracles of that day included a heavenly flame settling on each person's head and the ability to speak in unknown languages (Acts 2:1–13). We should note

1

that this was a communal miracle, unlike most miracles that were worked by a specific miracle worker upon a specific recipient.

Once things calmed down a bit, Jesus's disciple Peter apparently did some spectacular preaching. He told how Jesus had fulfilled prophecy and that the listeners must turn to God. The core of the sermon is unfortunately reduced to the simple summary that he "continued preaching for a long time, strongly urging all his listeners, 'Save yourselves from this generation that has gone astray!'" (Acts 2:40)

The twenty-six verses that Peter spoke leading up to this message would only have taken a few minutes to deliver—not a very long sermon by any standard. It appears that this recorded portion was only the warm-up, and not his main point. Whatever Peter said in that maddening gap must have been pretty compelling, because three thousand people converted on that day (Acts 2:41).

This is a very important sermon to reduce to a single sentence, and unfortunately the why and how of his core message was lost. We'll have to dig a bit to unearth the likely content of Peter's missing message. Fortunately, the Bible provides us with many clues about how the generation was understood to have gone astray. The most prominent clues came in the immediate reaction of those who believed, and followed the predecessor of Christianity, which was then known as the Way.

## NO POVERTY AMONG THEM

The first clue is found in the response of the believers. It quickly became clear that something very unusual was happening economically, as well as spiritually, as "all the believers met together constantly and shared everything they had. They sold their possessions and shared the proceeds with those in need." (Acts 2:44–45)

A resurrected divinity, eternal life for believers, and other elements of the emerging faith were fairly commonplace in the various religions and cults of that era, but this sharing was a key feature that set the Way apart.

In *Velvet Elvis*, Rob Bell makes the point that inspired me to investigate the connection between Christ and cooperative organizing: "To try to prove there was an empty tomb wouldn't have gotten very far with the average citizen of the Roman Empire; they had heard it all before. This is why so many passages about the early church deal with possessions and meals and generosity."[1]

This emphasis on experience over argument was what gave the Way an edge over competing religions of the day, and the experience itself was dramatic: "There was no poverty among them, because people who owned land or houses sold them and brought the money to the apostles to give to others in need" (Acts 4:34–35). A new society was bursting onto the scene, with an open invitation for anyone to join.

What are we to make of this behavior? On the one hand, these early followers of Jesus were living in a very different situation from our own. A small religious group facing persecution in the wake of its leader's execution would likely pull together to face a threatening future, and there are many historic and contemporary examples of communally organized sects. On the other hand, it wasn't written that they shared a forced and fearful communist rule that made everyone poor, or that the poor among them suffered less than poor people outside the community.

There was simply no poverty among them.

This sharing is certainly one of the reasons why followers of the Way were persecuted, and one of the reasons why their movement grew in spite of persecution. Their communal organization threatened a society based on distinct classes and power structures. They didn't directly challenge the institution of slavery, but they undermined the system just the same: believers who were part of a community with no poverty would have no fear of having to become slaves to support themselves. More provocative still, their allegiance was to God and each other, and not to Caesar.

The spread of this movement was a challenge to the economic order of the day; as such challenges often do, it provoked a violent response. The worldly powers had no control over the early Christians beyond physical force, and so that was how the powers responded.

Acts chapter 5 provides a clear indication that this sharing was a development of great spiritual importance. We had been told that many members gave what they had, with great results (Acts 4:34–35). This giving was highly regarded. However,

> There was also a man named Ananias who, with his wife Sapphira,
> sold some property. He brought part of the money to the apostles

1. Bell, *Velvet Elvis*, 164.

but he claimed it was the full amount. His wife had agreed to the deception.

Then Peter said, "Ananias, why has Satan filled your heart? You lied to the Holy Spirit, and you kept some of the money for yourself. The property was yours to sell or not sell, as you wished. And after selling it, the money was yours to give away. How could you do a thing like this? You weren't lying to us but to God."

As soon as Ananias heard these words, he fell to the floor and died. Everyone who heard about it was terrified. Then some young men wrapped him in a sheet and took him out and buried him."

About three hours later his wife came in, not knowing what had happened. Peter asked her, "Was this the price you and your husband received for your land?"

"Yes," she replied, "that was the price."

And Peter said, "How could the two of you even think of do-ing a thing like this—conspiring together to test the Spirit of the Lord? Just outside that door are the young men who buried your husband, and they will carry you out, too."

Instantly, she fell to the floor and died. When the young men came in and saw that she was dead, they carried her out and bur-ied her beside her husband. Great fear gripped the entire church and all others who heard what had happened. (Acts 5:1–10)

The two were struck dead on the spot—the only New Testament characters to receive such immediate and severe punishment. Even Herod died of a specific ailment over time (Acts 12:23), and Judas lived to com-mit suicide (Matt 27:1–5). Stranger still, Ananias and Sapphira are smit-ten for violating a rule that was not even a requirement! In the midst of telling them how badly they had sinned, Peter reminds us that the whole arrangement was voluntary.

The story of Ananias and Sapphira is often cited as an illustration of why it is bad to lie, but the lesson of punishment by death could have been delivered for any number of offenses—adultery, theft, or simple dis-honesty about one's true level of faith. It is unlikely that this was the only lie told during this period. Peter himself had thrice denied knowing Jesus (John 18:15–27).

The most extreme punishments were reserved for being uncoop-erative—for undermining the system that was having such spectacu-lar results in carrying out Jesus's social teachings. The story of Ananias and Sapphira shows us what happens when someone is not forthcoming about what they have to offer. These two were hypocrites who wanted recognition that they didn't deserve.

What are we to make of all this? Clearly there was some sort of fervor in the movement to follow this new Messiah, and whatever Peter said on Pentecost gave clear direction toward widespread voluntary communal organizing. Even though it was not necessary to give up one's property to join, there seems to have been considerable desire to do so.

## MAKING IT WORK

Voluntary communal organizing has something of a mixed reputation. It does not always go smoothly, especially when there are people involved. Throwing resources into a common pot is challenging even among small and uniform groups with a stable membership, and one might expect difficulties to arise in this large and rapidly growing movement, which faced all sorts of internal and external challenges.

Sure enough, in the very next chapter of Acts, ethnic divisions begin to develop between the Greeks and Hebrews about the distribution of food. The harmony was disturbed and the apostles had to act.

> So the Twelve called a meeting of all the believers. "We apostles should spend our time preaching and teaching the word of God, not administering a food program," they said. "Now look around among yourselves, brothers, and select seven men who are well respected and are full of the Holy Spirit and wisdom. We will put them in charge of this business. Then we can spend our time in prayer and preaching and teaching the word." (Acts 6:2–4)

It is important to note that they called for the election of seven leaders, who were also called servants or deacons. The pooling of resources was a continuation of something that had existed within Jesus's inner circle, in which Judas had acted as treasurer. Concern with how poorly Judas had turned out may have added to the urge for sharing the particularly tempting responsibility of managing the money.

Whatever the apostles were thinking, group leadership quickly proved to be a wise move. The list of deacons begins with Stephen, who is described as being "full of faith and the Holy Spirit." (Acts 6:5) Presumably he would have won the election if there had been only a single position, but fortunately he was only one member of this leadership team, since he was soon arrested and executed. If he had been in a position of unique power, they would have had to start from scratch. By raising up a group of leaders, the believers had strengthened their hand considerably.

The spiritual leadership was chosen by God, but the apostles realized that their responsibilities were of the spirit and not of the purse. Perhaps motivated by Jesus's encouragement to "give to Caesar what belongs to him" (Matt 22:21) or by the memory of how driving the merchants from the temple (John 2:15–16) was the only time that Jesus was impassioned enough to use force, they created a separation of powers.

The apostles avoided involvement with financial management, which had to be accountable to the whole community. Furthermore, the control was not given to those who brought more resources to the table, as is usually done in the modern business world. Power was shared among *all the believers.*

One more passage is of particular interest. A division developed between those who thought that the Jewish law still applied, and those who thought that Jesus had released them from following the law. This division came to a head over the question of circumcision. When some former Pharisees began preaching that circumcision was necessary, Paul and Barnabas took the opposite position.

This dispute eventually led to what is known as the Council of Jerusalem (Acts 15). The biblical account records several steps to the deliberation. First, "the apostles and elders got together to decide this question. At the meeting, after a long discussion," they decided to drop the rule on circumcision (vv. 6–7). Peter issued a closing statement and there "was no further discussion" (v. 12). "Then the apostles and elders and the whole church in Jerusalem chose delegates, and they sent them to Antioch of Syria with Paul and Barnabas to report this decision" (v. 22).

This decision was made by the church leadership and relayed by delegates chosen by the whole gathering. Their message to those not present contained an interesting choice of words that cast light on how the leaders saw their decision. The message began by saying that "it seemed good to us, having unanimously agreed on our decision, to send you these official representatives" (Acts 15:25).

"Seemed" indicates a certain level of humility and an admission that they might not have grasped an absolute truth. Their conclusion reiterated their humility with a limited set of rules that left most questions open for local decisions: "You must abstain from eating food offered to idols, from consuming blood or eating the meat of strangled animals, and from sexual immorality. If you do this, you will do well" (Acts 15:29).

The question of circumcision was a theological question, and not directly related to the economic and organizational issues on which this book is focused. However, the way in which this issue was handled gives insight into how major decisions were made and provides us with some indication of how the early church functioned. Decisions made in a way that involved the whole community, and leadership was chosen by an inclusive process.

We have already seen how this was the case for deacons and delegates, but even the selection of apostles was inclusive. Eleven of the apostles were chosen directly by Jesus, but they were special cases, and some new process was obviously needed to deal with their inevitable retirement or death. Judas's replacement shows that this process was highly inclusive.

"They all met together continually for prayer, along with Mary, the mother of Jesus, several other women, and the brothers of Jesus. During this time, on a day when about 120 believers were present" (Acts 1:14–5), Peter led a process by which they narrowed down their choices to two candidates, and "then they cast lots, and in this way Matthias was chosen and became an apostle with the other eleven" (Acts 1:26). The final selection was left to God through the casting of lots, but the names in the proverbial hat were chosen by the whole. The meeting leader's role was that of a facilitator.

## CONNECTING THE DOTS

From the start, the Way presented a distinct alternative to the Roman order, which so closely resembles our own modern order. This is a very inconvenient insight, since fully embracing these examples would require major restructuring of both church and economy. These passages are often ignored or dismissed as something that was not central to the message of the story. After all, it is argued, God doesn't say that this is the only way to do things, right?

Well, not exactly.

When one reads the Bible with an eye for teachings about how people ought to organize, there are some pretty clear patterns about what works well and is pleasing to God. There are also clear messages about what doesn't work well and tends to make God angry. We can see that the practices of the Way were strongly rooted in the prophetic tradition.

As we dig deeper, we shall see that the story told in Acts continues a story that is as old as Adam and Eve. This story runs in a strong thread through the history of Israel from a point immediately before the receipt of the Ten Commandments, which would not have happened without cooperation. This thread continues through the unfortunate leadership transition from Judges to Kings, through Israel's subsequent collapse and Nehemiah's servant leadership during the rebuilding of Jerusalem. Many of the prophets preach the message of cooperation. Even God reveals a collaborative streak at times, taking feedback from Moses and others, and even calling a meeting of the spirits to seek help in one case (2 Chr 18:18–21).

Christianity is often understood to be a personal matter of one's relationship with God, and attempts to bring that relationship into the public sphere have often been viewed as threats to our secular social order. This is a curious state of affairs for the followers of a faith that erupted out a struggle for collective liberation against an oppressive empire, which in turn grew out of the Jewish nation's efforts to identify itself. The modern understanding of individual salvation would have sounded strange to Jesus's first followers.

The Way was apparently an attempt to build a heavenly society in eager anticipation of Christ's imminent return. The believers understood that they had work to do. They had to get the house ready for the master's return, so to speak. In order to reach the potential glimpsed by the first believers, I believe that the modern followers of Jesus need to rediscover whatever it was that had everyone so filled with the Spirit back then.

We need to reclaim Jesus's message of liberation and transformation in a way that the world can see. We need to stop talking about love and start showing it in ways that go beyond individual acts of kindness. Cooperation is not a substitute for spiritual growth or redemption; it is a way to nurture the behaviors that support them.

Most churchgoers are told each Sunday to avoid sin, and then are sent back out into a world that is based in greed and envy and wrath. We need to find ways of organizing outside of church, of carrying our beliefs over to Monday morning. We hear a message of liberation and love that remains hollow and abstract in the face of growing government oppression, warfare, and systematic global trade that allows us to effortlessly sin against the world's poor without even knowing that we are doing it.

As old ways disintegrate, great new growth is happening. This break-down is political, economic, and spiritual; and a new message of hope is urgently needed. Jesus directly addressed our needs amid this social collapse, but the traditional way of looking at church prevents the Bible's messages from reaching their full potential as a clarion call of tangible liberation.

These days, the world's powers are so strong that it is easy to lose hope that things can change, and difficult to know where to start. Our current affairs are bad enough that even the most rationalist unbeliever might yearn for divine intervention.

We need a miracle—a big one.

Fortunately the Bible provides a roadmap of sorts in its descrip-tion of how the first followers of the risen Jesus behaved. They organized in a way that has much in common with the modern form of business known as cooperatives, or co-ops. In essence, the first seven leaders were a democratically elected board of directors.

## COOPERATIVES EXPLAINED

Biblical cooperation can be found in the communal monasticism of the Egyptian deserts, in European peasant communes from medieval times through the Industrial Revolution, and in the utopian communities of early American history. It continues today through traditions like those of the Hutterites, through large cooperative economic systems in Spain and Italy, and through Latin American base communities. Faith-based communities, credit unions and other cooperatives exist throughout of the world.

To see what all these groups have in common with each other, it will be helpful to have a general understanding of cooperatives. The In-ternational Cooperative Alliance gives the following definition: "A co-operative is an autonomous association of persons united voluntarily to meet their common economic, social, and cultural needs and aspirations through a jointly-owned and democratically-controlled enterprise."[2]

---

2. International Cooperative Alliance, "Cooperative Identity."

Cooperatives can be applied in many ways, and most are not specifically faith-based. They mesh well with Christian values by providing a tangible way to love one's neighbor, but they are not a Christian movement and generally cherish openness to people of all faiths.

Some cooperatives are household names. Best Western hotels are the results of independent hotels banding together cooperatively. Ocean Spray is an industry leader for cranberry growers. The Associated Press is a cooperative formed by newspapers to share reporting resources. True Value helps small businesses stay alive in the face of growing threats from big box stores.

Co-ops may look like regular businesses, but rather than giving power to those with the largest financial investment, power is shared democratically on the basis of one vote per member. They operate for the benefit of those who own and use them, whether users are shoppers, workers, farmers, or small-business owners. Co-ops provide banking, babysitting, housing, employment, insurance, and funerals. They refine oil, manufacture appliances and vehicles, and participate in all aspects of getting food from the farm to dinner table. Wherever the market fails to meet the needs of people, cooperatives can be found.

Co-ops have a broad appeal. Their members include ranchers in Oregon, bike messengers in Berkeley, farmers in Alabama, home-schoolers in Idaho, and apartment dwellers in Manhattan. Co-ops can be small, informal, food-buying clubs or Fortune 500 companies. Thirty percent of produce grown in the United States passes through at least one co-op on its way to market. Ten thousand credit unions collectively have 84 million members and $600 billion in assets. Cooperatives provide homes for 1.5 million people. More than 75 percent of the nation's land is served by cooperative utilities, which were organized in response to the private sector's failure to serve our less-dense rural populations.

In all, nearly half of Americans are co-op members.[3]

Cooperatives are found throughout the world, and in some countries the movement is much stronger than here in the United States. I don't wish to minimize the accomplishments elsewhere, but because I am an American writing primarily for a domestic audience, I will generally use examples from the U.S. I will also use several international models because they do not have counterparts in this country. There are places

3. National Cooperative Business Association, "Co-op Statistics."

that are further along in developing cooperative economies, and those models are essential for our consideration. They will help debunk the myth that our greed-based economy is the only way of doing things.

Faith-based cooperation is not unique to Christianity. Jewish communes called kibbutzim and Islamic mutual insurance companies are only two examples of how other religions have cooperative values. This common value provides an important opportunity for reconciliation in our troubled times.

I will use "cooperative" (or "co-op") as a noun to describe organizations that identify themselves by that term. However, there is not a total similarity between cooperatives and the related organizations created out of Christian inspiration. Therefore in many cases, I will describe organizations with the adjective "cooperative." In many cases these organizations will be slightly (or significantly) different from modern co-ops.

Having said all that, there are many cooperative organizations rooted in Jesus's teachings. Some of these are small and fairly simple, such as the Christian intentional communities that are currently springing up around the country. These are made up of one or several households of people who have committed to collectively model their lives after Christ. Many of these are affiliated with movements such as the Catholic Workers or the New Monasticism.

Other forms of cooperation look more like businesses. There are many faith-based credit unions, cooperative health-care arrangements, food-distribution cooperatives, and others. Some cooperative ministries combine living in community with working in collectively owned enterprises. For example, Jesus People USA is based in a large apartment complex in Chicago and has several businesses that bring income to the community.

Also, many cooperatives started as religious efforts but have moved away from a clearly spiritual mission in order to be more inclusive and help more people. In many cases, members may not even know the co-op's spiritual origins. This loss of focus may be seen as a setback, but these cooperatives are still pulling at least in a direction that is supported by biblical teachings.

Some cooperative efforts are quite large. The most famous is Mondragon, which provides employment to more than eighty thousand people in the Basque country of northern Spain. It has developed into a relatively autonomous economic system and provides education, health care, and cradle-to-grave social security for all its members. It began as a small manufacturer of household appliances and is now an economic powerhouse that owns one of Spain's largest banks and the nation's largest domestically owned grocery-store chains—all under democratic control by members who join of their own free will.[4]

Mondragon is the world's most developed cooperative economy, but it is hardly the largest in terms of membership. Desjardins is a faith-based cooperative movement in French Canada with nearly six million members and forty thousand employees working at nearly a thousand credit unions. This huge cooperative system provides an example of how a project that grew out of Christian values can have a major impact and can build to a great size while maintaining decentralized control. This is an example of what is called a cooperative federation, in which many independent co-ops join together to create services that they couldn't achieve alone.[5]

Even more massive in terms of its social impact is the Confederazione Cooperative Italiane, which is made up of more than 18,500 separate cooperatives. These cooperatives collectively have nearly three million members, four hundred thousand employees, and 40 billion euros in annual sales.[6] Desjardins and the Confederazione show how cooperatives can break out into the whole economy.

## COOPERATIVE DISAGREEMENT

Italy also provides a tantalizing clue about how helpful cooperatives can truly be in a pluralist society like ours. The United States is severely divided about some areas of government policy, and cooperatives may help take pressure off government so that it can focus it on points of agreement.

The Confederazione is not alone in Italy. That nation is home to several different cooperative federations that provide jobs and services to millions of people. They each have different philosophies and values, but they are all cooperative in nature. They do not always get along, but they are able to coexist. The Italians show us that it is possible to cre-

4. Mondragon Cooperación Cooperativa. "Most Relevant Data"; see also Morrison, *We Build the Road.*

5. Desjardins, "Desjardins Figures."

6. Confederazione, "Global Figures."

ate parallel, values-based systems that are large, complex, and voluntary. Rather than trying to cram our ideas down the throats of those who have different values, we can develop cooperative enterprises among people with common ethical backgrounds.

The United States faces a number of issues and values around which there is a growing consensus across political and religious boundaries. In some cases there is a difference in language and end goals, but this does not lessen the compatibility of the intermediate goals and the public policy required. For example, "environmentalism" and "creation care" are similar concepts in terms of how they manifest as government policy, and both require us to live on the earth in less destructive ways.

It may be appropriate for governments to regulate such cases of general agreement, where a clear majority shares compatible goals. However, regulation becomes tyranny when there is strong disagreement. In such cases where there is no chance for consensus—such as defining "family" in order to determine health insurance coverage—the government should step aside and encourage cooperation.

In some ways, this scenario resembles privatization or encouragement of business development, but with a very important distinction: Cooperative firms must be democratically controlled by those who use their services. Cooperatives can capture the ideals of community and social justice within a market economy. They contain the best of both worlds.

We are called to move beyond the divisiveness that has plagued our nation, and to find ways to work together cooperatively with those who share our values. We must let go of forcing our wills on each other, and get back to the spirit of liberty that got people excited about American independence in the first place. This same spirit is found throughout the Bible.

*two*

# JUDGES AND KINGS

## THE OLD TESTAMENT'S TALE OF LEADERS AND RULERS

The Old Testament is full of prophets and kings telling people what to do, and it might not seem to be a model of equality and empowerment. Nevertheless, we can make out the foundation for the teachings of Jesus and the acts of his followers.

When we look at organization throughout the Old Testament, we see two patterns: First, when power is concentrated in the hands of a single ruler, things tend to go worse than when power is spread out among the people. Second, God prefers that we treat each other justly and often becomes angry when this does not happen. These lessons shine through most clearly when we look at how the people implement the law. Many books have been written about the content of God's will, so I would like to keep the focus on how that will is carried out.

The history of Israel was much like that of a family, complete with references to its fathers and even to a mother. Moses played a very strong patriarchal role at first, but as the story progressed, the nation matured toward equality, while Moses's role became less central. This was much like the way children gain responsibility as they grow into adults. There were definitely strong leaders throughout the story, but also a clear progression toward a more cooperative way of leading that reached its peak in Jesus's servant leadership.

This cooperation begins in Genesis.

## WORKING WITH GOD

For the first five days of creation, God worked alone. God called into being the earth, the waters, the land, the skies, the plants, and the animals. It was good, but God took a different approach when it came time to create humans.

God said, "Let us make people in our image, to be like ourselves" (Gen 1:26). Many Bible translations use the noun "man," but the act and actors were clearly plural. Before this point God simply created, but when it came to creating God's own reflection, it was declared an act of collaboration. It is almost as though God had a meeting of the Trinity and made a proposal. We cannot escape God's clear plurality in this verse, and the implication that Adam and Eve were God's image together. If we are to act as though we are in God's image, we too must work together in harmony.

God's collaborative side also shows up in several passages that recount how God was convinced to relent after making a declaration: Abraham haggled with God about how many innocents must be found in Sodom for the city to be spared (Gen 19:23–32). Moses convinced God to share his leadership burden with Aaron, even though this was clearly not God's will (Exod 4:10–17). Moses twice convinced God to not destroy Israel after God had already stated an intention to do so (Exod 32:9–14, Num 14:11–20). This also happened on a personal level, when Ezekiel negotiated with God and talked his way out of following one of God's commands. (Ezek 4:14–5)

These can be dismissed as signs of God's forgiveness, but the most interesting story of divine yielding describes a prophetic vision in which God asks for help from the spirits who have assembled:

> "Who can entice King Ahab of Israel to go into battle against Ramoth-gilead so that he can be killed there?" There were many suggestions, until finally a spirit approached the Lord and said "I can do it!"
>
> "How will you do this?" the Lord asked.
>
> And the spirit replied, "I will go out and inspire all of Ahab's prophets to speak lies."
>
> "You will succeed," said the Lord. "Go ahead and do it."
> (2 Chr 18:19–21)

God certainly didn't need help, and could have simply wiped Ahab off the face of the earth. However, God took a cooperative approach and sought suggestions. It was still God's decision, but power was shared, both in development and implementation of the plan. God's desire for cooperation makes many more appearances.

### THE BEGINNINGS OF ISRAEL

The book of Exodus describes the birth and childhood of Israel as a nation. Moses is often portrayed as a father figure who dictated God's will, but the Bible records that it did not take long for this newborn society to develop some diffusion of responsibility.

We have already noted that Moses and Aaron split the leadership duties of prophet and priest, but God's desire for cooperation became even clearer once the exodus was underway. Two events clearly establish that God didn't mean for Moses to lead Israel alone.

The first event occurred soon after the Israelites left Egypt for their long desert sojourn. After God had taken care of the people's need for food and water, they were attacked by the Amalekites. Moses watched from a nearby hill as the battle began:

> As long as Moses held up the staff with his hands, the Israelites had the advantage. But whenever he lowered his hands, the Amalekites gained the upper hand. Moses' arms finally became too tired to hold up the staff any longer. So Aaron and Hur found a stone for him to sit on. Then they stood on each side, holding up his hands until sunset. As a result, Joshua and his troops were able to crush the army of Amalek. (Exod 17:11–13)

This was a humbling lesson to Moses that he couldn't shoulder the burden of leadership by himself. But it seems that he did not immediately get the point, so God tried again using a more explicit message from a human source. Moses's father-in-law, Jethro, came for a visit.

> When Moses' father-in-law saw all that Moses was doing for the people, he said, "Why are you trying to do this alone? The people have been standing here all day to get your help."
>
> Moses replied, "Well, the people come to me to seek God's guidance. When an argument arises, I am the one who settles the case. I inform the people of God's decisions and teach them his laws and instructions.

"This is not good!" his father-in-law exclaimed. "You're going to wear yourself out—and the people too. This job is too heavy a burden for you to handle by yourself. Now let me give you a word of advice, and may God be with you. You should continue to be the people's representative before God, bringing him their questions to be decided. You should tell them God's decisions, teach them God's laws and instructions, and show them how to conduct their lives. But find some capable, honest men who fear God and hate bribes. Appoint them as judges over groups of one thousand, one hundred, fifty and ten. These men can serve the people, resolving all the ordinary cases. Anything that is too important or too complicated can be brought to you. But they can take care of the smaller matters themselves. They will help you carry the load, making the task easier for you." (Exod 18:14–22)

We later learn that these judges were selected by the people and are given clear instructions not to discriminate against foreigners or the poor (Deut 1:9–18).

There is no direct description of how this worked out beyond a statement that this recommendation was implemented. The most striking result was that once Moses was freed from acting as judge from dawn to dusk, he became more available for God's other business. Once Moses got help, he was able to go up the mountain, and God promptly delivered the Ten Commandments. The rest is history.

These stories provide a stark warning against having a single leader hold all the power and responsibility. It is well known that the details and routine of a busy life will get in the way of one's spiritual growth, and this passage emphasizes the need for delegation of responsibility.

God still preferred to have one person in charge during this phase of Israel's development. The delegation was for routine cases, which would be referred back to Moses as needed. Moses was still in charge. As we shall see, this was the beginning of a long process of distributing power that mirrors the way that responsibility is passed from one generation to the next.

Parents need to keep their young children under control until they can develop more sense and responsibility. Good decisions are rewarded with more responsibility until adult decisions are possible. Of course, every parent knows that kids rebel, which is a time-honored way of testing out the rules. When this happens, it is important to be clear and consistent in maintaining boundaries. Not surprisingly, God showed a firm hand in response to Korah's rebellion.

In this story, the rebels' grievance did not seem to be in response to a particular decision but was a reaction to Moses's power itself: "You have gone too far! Everyone in Israel has been set apart by the Lord, and he is with all of us. What right do you have to act as though you are greater than anyone else among all these people of the Lord?" (Num 16:3).

It seems that Moses must have had some right to act in this regard, since the story ends with the rebels' being swallowed up by the earth and with a plague finishing off thousands of their relatives. It was clear that the Israelites were not yet ready for popular rule.

This could be interpreted as an indication that God only wants one person in charge, but we must remember that the rebels were popular leaders. This was a substantial uprising in which the conspirators involved "250 other prominent leaders, all members of the assembly" (Num 16:2). The rebels were within their rights to participate in the nation's governance, but as Moses responded, "You Levites are the ones who have gone too far!" (Num 16:7).

The problem may have been the clumsy way that the rebels had raised their concerns. Jethro brought his suggestion discreetly, but it seems that Korah and his collaborators just dumped it all out in the open. Crisis demands strong leadership, and the precarious situation in which the Israelites found themselves demanded strong leadership indeed. There was no room for extracurricular squabbling, so the rebels' punishment could also be interpreted as God telling the kids to settle down, to stop squabbling.

### MORE THAN ENOUGH

Another cooperative theme that appears during the exodus is that of voluntary contribution.

Building the tabernacle was a very important task with extremely detailed and specific directions. Much work was needed, but it was done without forced labor or contributions: "If their hearts were stirred and they desired to do so, they brought to the Lord their offerings of materials for the Tabernacle and its furnishings and for the holy garments" (Exod 35:20).

This sort of arrangement is often dismissed as idealistic, but in this case it worked well. After a short period of effort, "this message was sent throughout the camp: 'Bring no more materials! You have already brought more than enough.' So the people stopped bringing their offerings. Their contributions were more than enough to complete the whole project" (Exod 36:6–7).

We see that if a project is worthwhile and has popular support, rigid enforcement should not be necessary. If God wants something to happen, there should be no need for people to force each other to do it.

This informal sharing of burdens depended on wealth's being distributed equally, so there was also sharing of income. When the Israelites were victorious in battle, all shared in the benefit. God instructed them to "then divide the plunder into two parts and give half to the men who fought the battle, and half to the rest of the people" (Num 31:27). This maintained a balance between the need to reward hard work and the need to make sure that wealth is shared.

Sharing also occurred on a larger scale. The clans that made up each tribe began with sufficient resources when they finally arrived in the Promised Land. They were instructed to divide the land among the clans "by sacred lot and in proportion to their size" (Num 33:54). To maintain this fairness, women who were in line to inherit land were not allowed to marry outside of their clans. "No inheritance may pass from one tribe to another; each tribe of Israel must hold on to its allotted inheritance" (Num 36:9).

## JUDGES AND KINGS

After Moses died, leadership passed to the military leader Joshua, who oversaw the Israelite conquest of the Holy Land. Without Moses's spiritual leadership, the Israelites went astray, worshiped idols, and were conquered. Later God raised up a series of judges to lead them, and these leaders provide us with essential insight into how power should be handled.

Sometimes Israel had to make do without such wise and able leadership, which illustrated the important role of judges: "Whenever the Lord placed a judge over Israel, he was with that judge and rescued the people from their enemies throughout that judge's lifetime. For the Lord took pity on his people, who were burdened by oppression and suffering. But when the judge died, the people returned to their corrupt ways, behaving worse than those who had lived before them." (Judg 2:18–19)

Leadership by judges did not always work perfectly, but there was a clear contrast with the troubled period of rule by kings that followed. Kings often brought divisiveness, oppression, and violence. In some cases kings lived up to their responsibilities, but more often they did not.

The key difference between judges and kings can be drawn from a statement found in several places throughout the narrative, that "in those days Israel had no king, so the people did whatever seemed right in their own eyes" (Judg 17:6, 19:1, 21:25).

The judge filled an organic role, which provided leadership without hardening into a position that controlled the daily affairs of governance. Even though things went better when there was a judge than when there was not, it was not an essential administrative position that had hardened into an institution of its own. There was no clear line of succession with judges, who were divinely appointed. They came from all ranks of society and even included a woman named Deborah, who freed Israel from another period of subjugation and oversaw forty years of peace (Judg 4–5).

The judge was not a ruler, which is shown by one judge's response when asked to establish hereditary rule:

"Then the Israelites said to Gideon, 'Be our ruler! You and your son and your grandson will be our rulers, for you have rescued us from Midian.' But Gideon replied, 'I will not rule over you, nor will my son. The Lord will rule over you!'" (Judg 8:22–23).

Despite Gideon's protest, he was succeeded by an illegitimate son. This son, named Abimelech, killed all but one of his seventy half brothers in a blatant power grab, which played on family loyalty among his mother's relatives in Shechem. He was then declared to be king (Judg 9:1–6).

The surviving brother, Jotham, warned of a creeping monarchy, with a parable of the trees seeking a king: They first approached the olive tree, fig tree, and grapevine, and each declined the position in order to focus on doing useful work. Finally, they approached the thornbush, who was happy to take the throne (Judg 9:7–21).

This tale warned that even a popular ruler is not necessarily a good one. It also suggests that anyone who wants to be king should not be trusted with the job. Soon thereafter, we find that a popularly chosen leader does not have a permanent mandate.

After a few years, "God stirred up trouble between Abimelech and the people of Shechem, and they revolted. In the events that followed, God punished Abimelech and the men of Shechem for murdering Gideon's seventy sons." (Judg 9:23–24)

Here God played a major role in overthrowing a leader, which contradicts the common notion that rulers should not be challenged because God put them there. The uprising against Abimelech shows that God creates resistance as well as government. Despite this lesson, the judges' days were numbered.

The transition from judges to kings is critical for our understanding of power because it illustrates the difference between leaders and rulers. Leaders provide initiation and coordination, which is essential for any organization. Rulers tend to have negative impacts on how well people get along, and we shall see that God doesn't like them.

The era of judges gave way to kingship when the judge Samuel retired. He appointed his sons as his successors, but they turned out to be corrupt. As a result, the people asked Samuel for a king in order to be like the other nations. God was clearly not happy to hear of this request when Samuel told him of it, and warned that they would regret the change.

> "Do as they say," the Lord replied, "for it is me they are rejecting, not you. They don't want me to be their king any longer. Ever since I brought them from Egypt they have continually forsaken me and followed other gods. And now they are giving you the same treatment. Do as they ask, but solemnly warn them about the way a king will treat them."
>
> So Samuel passed on the Lord's warning to the people who were asking him for a king. "This is how a king will treat you," Samuel said. "The king will draft your sons and make them run before his chariots. Some will be commanders of his troops, while others will be slave laborers. Some will be forced to plow his fields and harvest his crops, while other will make his weapons and chariot equipment. The king will take your daughters from you and force them to cook and bake and make perfumes for him. He will take away the best of your fields and vineyards and olive groves and give them to his own servants. He will take a tenth of your harvest and distribute it among his officers and attendants. He will want your male and female slaves and demand the finest of your cattle and donkeys for his own use. He will demand a tenth of your flocks and you will be his slaves. When that day

Isaiah's focus on justice was clear from the first chapter of the book bearing his name, in which he described God's preference for justice over ritual.

> From now on, when you lift your hands in prayer, I will refuse to look. Even though you offer many prayers, I will not listen. For your hands are covered with the blood of your innocent victims. Wash yourselves and be clean! Let me no longer see your evil deeds. Give up your wicked ways. Learn to do good. Seek justice. Help the oppressed. Defend the orphan. Fight for the rights of widows. (Isa 1:16–17)

Amos also emphasized the importance of social justice. He echoed Isaiah's demands for doing good instead of relying on ritual and specified that unjust behavior was the greatest portion of Israel's collective sin.

> This is what the Lord says: "The people of Israel have sinned again and again, and I will not forget it. I will not let them go unpunished any longer! They have perverted justice by selling honest people for silver and poor people for a pair of sandals. They trample helpless people in the dust, and deny justice to those who are oppressed. Both father and son sleep with the same woman, corrupting my holy name. At their religious festivals, they lounge around in clothing stolen from their debtors. In the house of their god, they present offerings of wine purchased with stolen money." (Amos 2:6–8)

Hosea, Micah, Jeremiah, and Habakkuk also prophesied with strong emphasis on justice, but the work of all these prophets turned out to be in vain. As is often the case, the people ignored their personal contributions to the collective injustice and maintained business as usual. Division, corruption, and infighting continued in both kingdoms—and sometimes between them—until Jerusalem was finally destroyed by the Babylonians.

Being driven from one's home is difficult under any circumstances. But for the people of Judah, there was an added affront: God had specifically promised them the land from which they were now exiled, so this was a sign of profound religious failure. God's city then lay in ruins for generations as God's chosen people were exiled to the decadent merchant empire of Babylon. Clearly something had gone seriously wrong.

Ezekiel was a prophet of the exile who continued to preach that injustice was a major part of the reason for the predicament. He also looked toward the future and described at length the rules for the governance of a restored nation. His prophecies set clear limits on what princes could ask of the people (Ezek 45:7–25) and prohibited them from seizing land. (Ezek 46:18)

Ezekiel made no mention of a king's role. This subtle but curious omission suggests that the highest rank should be eliminated, or at least saved for God. Israel had already made the mistake of human kingship, and Ezekiel sought to prevent a repeat of this error.

Even after the Jewish people began to return from the exile, there was a continued emphasis on justice from the prophets Zechariah and Malachi. These later prophets sought to avoid a return to the ways that had proved so disastrous before. Malachi also warned that with the coming messiah, God would hold people accountable for their unjust acts. He wrote God's words: "At that time I will put you on trial. I will be a ready witness against all sorcerers and adulterers and liars. I will speak against those who cheat employees for their wages, who oppress widows and orphans, or who deprive the foreigners living among you of justice, for these people do not fear me" (Mal 3:5).

## REBUILDING JERUSALEM

The servant leadership, which Jesus would later model, makes a striking appearance in the historical book of Nehemiah, which includes an account of the rebuilding of the walls of Jerusalem. This restoration was a key event in bringing the Israelites back to the Holy Land, and was therefore among the most important events recorded in the Old Testament. The Bible provides a detailed description of the rebuilding process, so we may learn from how it was carried out.

The exile is commonly understood to have lasted seventy years, at which point the temple began to be rebuilt. Approximately one hundred years after Jerusalem's destruction, much of the city was still in ruins. The temple had been rebuilt, but it was without protection. There was nothing to ensure the safety and independence of the people who worshiped at that temple.

Nehemiah heard the news that the recovery had stalled and was then commissioned by God to rebuild the walls in a decentralized grassroots effort. It would have been much simpler for God to give this task to someone who was already in a position of authority, but God chose someone of common birth who was still in exile.

Nehemiah worked outside official channels and brought in the official leaders after he had already discerned a course of action. Fortunately the leaders saw the merit of this approach, and work quickly got under way (Neh 2:16–8). Nehemiah's genius was to organize groups of people to take care of the section of wall closest to them.

The occupying powers opposed the rebuilding effort, so there was a constant threat of attack. So the people engaged in a collective defense strategy in which people took turns working and standing guard. Defense had centralized coordination but was ultimately everyone's responsibility. There were no soldiers keeping watch as the people toiled (Neh 4:16–23).

The rebuilding effort was highly disruptive to the local economy and drove many people deeper into poverty. To address this, Nehemiah called a public meeting to hold the wealthy accountable and press for comprehensive debt relief:

> At the meeting [Nehemiah] said to them, "The rest of us are doing all we can to redeem our Jewish relatives who have had to sell themselves to pagan foreigners, but you are selling them back into slavery again. How often must we redeem them?' And they had nothing to say in their defense."
>
> Then [he] pressed further, "What you are doing is not right! . . . Repay the interest you charged on their money, grain, wine and olive oil."
>
> Then they replied, "We will give back everything and demand nothing of the people. We will do as you say." (Neh 5:8–12)

Nehemiah did take an official leadership position but used his own resources to provide the substantial hospitality that was part of his position. He recalled, "I asked for nothing, even though I regularly fed 150 Jewish officials at my table. . . . Yet I refused to claim the governor's food allowance because the people were already having a difficult time." (Neh 5:17–18)

Nehemiah teaches us the importance of grassroots leadership. The Judahite king had made a pact with the Babylonians and was unable to lead the effort to rebuild Jerusalem's defenses. It was therefore left to a decentralized community effort organized by a divinely inspired leader acting as first among equals. This was a grassroots project to the core and shows that the decentralized approach can be used for large, important, and complicated projects.

This decentralization is a key piece of the cooperative puzzle. There was unity of vision but the work was completed without micromanagement. The residents near each section of the wall worked together in ways that reflected who they were and what they had to contribute. Nehemiah 3 describes how the size of work crews varied, and it records that some crews were small enough that each individual's name was recorded. The sections built by a team varied from the width of a house to 1500 feet in length, while some teams worked on specific gates. Leadership positions did not directly relate to one's role in the rebuilding. In one case people worked without their leaders (Neh 3:5). In another, the leader of half the city worked in a team with his daughters (Neh 3:12).

The wall was built without a coordinated design, but the whole thing fit together somehow. In the same way, cooperatives can be brought together despite their uncoordinated origins. Central management is not necessary as long as there is unity of purpose.

The people rebuilt the wall in a spirit of equality and shared sacrifice and it took only fifty-two days to finish a job that had taken more than a century to begin (Neh 6:15). This was a miracle of cooperation, which provided a taste of what was to come.

These commandments are intertwined, for Jesus taught that we show our love for God through our treatment of others. Loving God and loving each other are two sides of the same coin.

## LOVE IN ACTION

Jesus warned that God takes our treatment of one another personally. He told a story in which God gives favor to the generous, declaring, "I was hungry and you fed me. I was thirsty and you gave me a drink. I was a stranger and you invited me into your home. . . . When you did it to the least of these my brothers and sisters, you were doing it to me!" (Matt 25:35–40).

We usually think of love as an internal state or an emotional attitude towards others. However, Jesus taught that action is needed when he said, "Your love for one another will prove to the world that you are my disciples" (John 13:35). One's emotional state is a poor proof of anything by itself; to convince the world, it must be accompanied by outward action.

Cooperation was hardly the only point of Jesus's ministry, but it was clearly of high importance. He was continuing a tradition of prophecy, which included a rich vein of protest against injustice.

This continuity is clear almost immediately. Luke recorded that Jesus's earliest public preaching included a quote of Isaiah: "The spirit of the Lord is upon me, for he has appointed me to preach Good News to the poor. He has sent me to proclaim that captives will be released, that the blind will see, that the downtrodden will be freed from their oppressors, and that the time of the Lord's favor has come" (Luke 4:18–19).

Luke also recalls that Jesus launches the Beatitudes with the words "God blesses you who are poor, for the Kingdom of God is given to you" (Luke 6:20).

Jesus also preached against oppression and was not even afraid of stirring things up within families: "Don't imagine that I came to bring peace to the earth! No, I came to bring a sword. I have come to set a man against his father, and a daughter against her mother, and a daughter-in-law against her mother-in-law" (Matt 10:34–5). This was not just division among family members; in each case he specifically provokes rebellion against the superiors of the family.

These examples alone show that Jesus was out for something different from the status quo of his day, or ours. The message was not primarily about individual behavior. Individual choices were essential, but within the context of how they strengthened or weakened the social fabric. Undermining the family might seem like an odd way to build community, but the hierarchies of the public sphere are all built upon habits learned in the family. People learn to take orders from their parents, first and foremost. This is useful in early life but becomes counterproductive in adulthood. Jesus must have recognized that there were deep-seated lessons to be unlearned.

Modern Christians might take issue with reading the Bible as an encouragement of social upheaval against the powerful, and may point to biblical writings that encourage obedience to the government. Jesus did not actively denounce slavery, and he mentioned it casually as though he saw it as part of the natural order of things.

Still, Jesus clearly and consistently presents a vision of radical equality, regardless of our various positions in the world (Mark 10:41–44). This does not rule out leadership or authority, but it is difficult to reconcile with an exclusive and sometimes wealthy ruler. Jesus didn't actively attack worldly rulers, but he also did little to lend them legitimacy.

## LESSONS IN SHARING

Economics and justice were major themes in Jesus's words and actions. These themes are highlighted in the way that Jesus often called disciples from their individual livelihoods to participate in a new and communal order. Rather than drawing people away from synagogues that failed to teach the right values, Jesus sought to incorporate those values into everyday life.

The Bible records a sharing of resources among Jesus's companions. This included common funds, which were placed in the care of Judas, even though it was known that he occasionally kept a bit for himself (John 12:6).

Jesus's most public miracles were of a social nature. John recorded that the first display of Jesus's glory was his turning water into wine at a wedding party. Not only did he make sure there was sufficient wine to keep the party going, he provided such an extreme abundance—more than one hundred gallons—that there was no longer any chance that the wine would run out (John 2:1–11). The scarcity that is the basis for financial value was eliminated, and so the participants were removed from the economy of exchange, transported into a gift economy.

He later fed the masses from very a small amount of loaves and fishes, with the same sort of excess left over. This miracle is described in all four New Testament Gospels, and twice by Mark and Matthew. One description records that five loaves and two fish fed five thousand men and their families, with twelve baskets to spare (Matt 14:15–21). These miracles were not only social but participatory. The abundance was not brought into existence in one sudden transformation, but grew as each person shared with the next.

Sharing worked both ways; labor, as well as the benefits from labor, needed to be shared. One description of the kingdom of heaven is the story of the ten bridesmaids (Matt 25:1–13): Five were wise and had plenty of oil for their lamps. However, these refused to share with the five foolish bridesmaids, who were unprepared. As a result, the foolish five had to run for more oil, and by the time they returned, the door to the wedding was locked.

This passage shows a need for balance between shared work and shared resources. There is a limit to sharing, and those who choose not to contribute shouldn't expect to be helped. The foolish bridesmaids were not poor or disabled. They simply didn't do their work.

This teaches an important part of any system based on sharing: Individuals must take personal responsibility, rather than taking advantage of others' generosity. Widows and children were often singled out for assistance because of their dependence, but those who were able to work should not have expected free handouts.

This need to take responsibility and work with whatever you have is further emphasized in the next passage, which is a story of three servants who are given money to invest. Two make wise choices and manage to double their shares, but a third simply buries the money to keep it safe. Their master replies: "To those who use well what they are given, even more will be given, and they will have an abundance. But from those who are unfaithful, even what little they have will be taken away" (Matt 25:29).

This passage is sometimes used to justify individual financial success, but that interpretation fits poorly into the overall context of Jesus's teachings. With the loaves and fishes, Jesus showed how letting go of a

scarce resource may have miraculous results. What better way to use resources well than to share them?

One of the Bible's best-known stories is that of the pious young
rich man who was told to give up his wealth and went away heartbroken
because he was not willing to do so. Jesus uses his failure in order to
teach others, declaring, "it is easier for a camel to go through the eye of
the needle than for a rich person to enter the Kingdom of God!" (Luke
18:25).

Sharing can seem threatening because it often involves giving up
our stuff. However, there is ample evidence that we are not meant to
hoard while others are in need. We often cling to our belongings like a
child frantically clutching a ball to prevent the other kids from getting it.
This very act of clutching prevents us from gaining any benefit from our
treasure.

Jesus addressed this by showing that accumulated possessions are
harmful to one's spiritual growth anyway, while giving them away is an
opportunity for great progress. There are many examples of this teaching
throughout the Gospels, but they are especially frequent in a few chapters
of the book of Luke.

One passage warns against accumulation of material things: "Yes, a
person is a fool to store up earthly wealth but not have a rich relationship
with God" (Luke 12:21). This might seem like two different issues, but we
should remember that Jesus also taught that our relationships with each
other are closely tied to our relationship with God because our treatment
of each other reflects our treatment of God. We can see how hoarding
wealth can get in the way.

Jesus elaborates on this a few verses later: "Sell your possessions and
give to those in need. . . . Wherever your treasure is, there your heart and
thoughts will also be" (Luke 12:33–34). Later in the Gospel, Jesus says,
"You cannot serve both God and money" (Luke 16:13).

What's more, he says that the very act of giving is beneficial: "I tell
you, use your worldly resources to benefit others and make friends. In
this way your generosity stores up a reward for you in heaven" (Luke
16:9).

It should be clear that the best way to use our resources well is not
to hold on to them but to send them out into the world, multiplying their
value. We may want to be comfortable, but the best way to do that is

through letting go. Our sharing will inspire others to share, which has the
potential to dramatically change the economic equation.

## LESSONS IN LEADERSHIP

Before he began his ministry, Jesus spent forty days in the desert being
tempted by the devil. He was tested three times, and the second test in
the Gospel of Luke immediately puts to rest any notion that God was out
to create a worldly kingdom: "Then the devil took him up and revealed
to him all the kingdoms of the world in a moment of time. The devil
told him, 'I will give you the glory of these kingdoms and authority over
them—because they are mine to give to anyone I please. I will give it all
to you if you bow down and worship me'" (Luke 4:5–7).

Jesus's refusal shows that we should be suspicious of those who want
to establish kingdoms—or democracies, for that matter—in God's name.
It was the devil who made that offer, and the devil who claimed the authority of the world.

Jesus refused to seize power but was often on the bad side of the
world's political and religious leaders. He did not directly attack them
and denied that he was trying to establish a worldly kingdom, but they
were still threatened. He had a different way of doing things, which left
those powers out of the loop.

Jesus did have an occasional stern word for powerful people, but
the rulers of the world were not his main concern. He seemed far more
interested in rooting out inequality among his followers:

> You know that in this world kings are tyrants and officials lord it
> over the people beneath them. But among you it should be quite
> different. Whoever wants to be a leader among you must first be
> your servant, and whoever wants to be first must become your
> slave. (Matt 20:25–27)

He also warns against raising people above their peers, and there was
no mistaking his intention that his followers treat each other as equals.

> Don't ever let anyone call you "Rabbi," for you have only one
> teacher, and all of you are on the same level with your brothers
> and sisters. And don't address anyone here on earth as "Father,"
> for only God in heaven is your spiritual Father. And don't let any-
> one call you "Master," for there is only one Master, the Messiah.

> The greatest among you must be a servant. But those who exalt
> themselves will be humbled, and those who humble themselves
> will be exalted. (Matt 23:10–12)

Again and again Jesus undermines the assumption that he is out
to overthrow the political order. He even actively avoided power at least
once. After feeding the multitudes, "Jesus saw they were ready to take
him by force and make him king, so he went higher into the hills alone"
(John 6:15).

John provides a further indication that Jesus's reign was not a part
of the current order. Jesus says, "I am not an earthly king. If I were, my
followers would have fought when I was arrested by the Jewish leaders.
But my Kingdom is not of this world" (John 18:36).

Jesus was so consistent in his refusal to take power, that Pilate found
him not guilty of any crime. Even so, Rome executed him at the demand
of the religious leaders. Pilate offered a choice of whom to free, and the
crowd chose to have Jesus executed (Matt 27:15–26). This was a con-
spicuous example of group decision making gone horribly awry; it shows
that the will of the people should not be imposed without careful discern-
ment. Mob rule is not God's will.

At the same time, many individual rulers who supposedly spoke for
God provided terrible leadership, so we can't take this single event as an
indication that inclusive decision making is bad.

## LESSONS IN DISCIPLINE

Over the years, one of the more difficult organizational problems has
been that of church discipline. Many denominations and churches have
split over disagreements about what to enforce and how to enforce it, yet
the Gospels give little support for enforcement of anything. Imagine how
much it would do for Christian unity if people didn't have the expecta-
tion that there is only one way to be Christian!

Jesus makes a comment that seems to indicate that we are judged by
our own standards rather than by a universal, impersonal morality. "Stop
judging others, and you will not be judged. Stop criticizing others, or it
will come back on you. If you forgive others, you will be forgiven" (Luke
6:37).

Forgiveness is a recurrent theme throughout the Gospels, but sometimes the focus is on how we expect to be forgiven by God rather than on how we must provide forgiveness to others. Jesus also says, "If another believer sins, rebuke him; then if he repents, forgive him. Even if he wrongs you seven times a day and each time turns again and asks forgiveness, forgive him" (Luke 17:3–4).

Jesus's actions provided an example of how morals should be maintained. His forgiveness was clear in the story of the woman who was to be stoned for committing adultery. Although she is caught red-handed, he saves her by demanding that the first stone be thrown by someone who is without sin. There was no such person and therefore no grounds for execution (John 8:1–11).

Jesus's most specific instructions on discipline provide opportunities for reconciliation at every step:

> If another believer sins against you, go privately and point out the fault. If the other person listens and confesses it, you have won that person back. But if you are unsuccessful, take one or two others with you and go back again, so that everything you say may be confirmed by two or three witnesses. If that person still refuses to listen, take your case to the church. If the church decides you are right, but the other person won't accept it, treat that person as a pagan or a corrupt tax collector. I tell you this: Whatever you prohibit on earth is prohibited in heaven, and whatever you allow on earth is allowed in heaven. (Matt 18:15–18)

This was Jesus's only surviving lesson about how a community should handle a member's sin, and it illustrates a sort of conflict resolution in which the offender must ultimately be persuaded that he or she is in the wrong. This process is not about sin in general but to be used for specific sin against the accuser. Some interpersonal harm is required for this procedure to be invoked.

If we take this passage seriously, the worst punishment is exclusion from the community. Expulsion is a tradition in many churches, but it is not a clearly biblical practice. The passage only says to treat the offender as a pagan or tax collector, so we must look to how undesirable people were treated.

Rather than excluding these undesirables, Jesus seemed to seek them out. Jesus often spent time with tax collectors, including his apostle

Matthew (Matt 9:9–13). After healing the Samaritan woman, he spent two days in her village even though Jews generally despised this ethnic group. His presence there resulted in many conversions (John 4:39–41).

Jesus also taught not to expel sinners because the act of expulsion causes further damage to the body. The story of the wheat and weeds illustrates this; it is a tale in which a farmer's enemy plants weeds among the crop. The farmer realizes that by pulling out the weeds, the crop would be harmed, and lets the weeds grow among the wheat (Matt 13:29–30).

Jesus also told stories of a lost sheep, a lost coin, and a wayward son (Luke 15:1–31). In each case the lost are sought and welcomed back. This should be no surprise, considering the consistency with which Jesus preached forgiveness and counseled us to avoid judging each other.

All of this does not quite fit with having a law to follow and punishment for violations. Of course, Jesus's message on the law was quite mixed. On the one hand he says, "Don't misunderstand why have come. I did not come to abolish the law of Moses or the writings of the prophets. No, I came to fulfill them" (Matt 5:17).

On the other hand, he declines to apply that law on several occasions: He saves the adulteress from execution (John 8:1–11), and when asked to rule on dividing an estate, he replies, "who made me a judge over you to decide things such as that?" (Luke 12:13–14). Jesus even makes a blanket statement against judgment: "If anyone hears me but does not obey me, I am not his judge—for I have come to save the world and not to judge it" (John 12:47).

If we are to follow Jesus, we should not judge one another. Nevertheless, the foundation of church discipline is judgment, loosening or binding certain acts. Based on Matt 16:18–19, for example, Roman Catholicism teaches that Jesus bestowed on Peter the authority to bind and loose—an authority now vested in the papacy.

Upon closer examination, the passage is ambiguous. The key statement lies between something Jesus clearly meant for Peter and something he clearly meant for the community.

> "Now I say to you that you are Peter, and upon this rock I build my church, and all the powers of hell will not conquer it. And I will give you the keys of the Kingdom of Heaven. Whatever you lock on earth will be locked in heaven, and whatever you open on earth will be opened in heaven." Then he sternly warned them not to tell anyone that he was the messiah. (Matt 16:18–20)

Jesus may have been speaking to Peter at that moment, but he did not say, "you and no other." As the next chapter will show, the rest of the New Testament teaches that these words were not taken to be for Peter alone.

*four*

# GUIDANCE FOR THE GATHERED

EXCAVATING THE ECCLESIA

The epistles are a series of letters that make up the largest part of the New Testament. Most were written during and about the period described in the book of Acts, and they provide a wealth of information about the communities of Christ's followers during the first century.

Each letter was directed at a specific church or individual regarding a specific situation. They were written by several different authors during a period spanning several decades, and thus provide several points of view from which events must be pieced together. They sometimes seem to contradict each other, and they were often written in response to a letter or event unknown to the modern world. What's more, the epistles are neither in chronological order nor evenly distributed in time and geography.

Therefore they do not provide a representative picture of things. Because of the complexity of these writings, one must be careful not to draw too many conclusions from any single passage. Even so, a general pattern of equality and voluntary sharing continues the traditions found in the rest of the Bible. We can also make out some surprising features of the Way.

The election of the seven deacons shows a clear distinction made between spiritual and economic leadership, but these servant leaders were not in charge of a separate organization (Acts 6:1–4). This may be because there wasn't a distinct church from which such a body could separate.

In this chapter I will point to examples from throughout the ecclesia. Some of these passages address activities now understood to be functions of a church, but I mean to apply them to more broadly. The integration of the ecclesia means that it is not always possible to separate out specific biblical guidance of how to run a church from general guidance for organizing other aspects of life. However, there is enough consistency that it seems safe to assume that these principles of equality, sharing, and liberty are intended for general application. We should be able to take any principles described in the epistles, and apply them to everyday life. It is absurd to think that God would want a liberated way of doing what we commonly think of as church embedded in an economy of inequality and poverty.

## NEITHER SLAVE NOR FREE

There is much in the epistles to support decentralized leadership. The first evidence can be found in their authors. Paul wrote most of the letters, although he never walked with Jesus and he joined the movement only after persecuting it severely. In contrast, tradition holds that the twelve official apostles wrote only a fraction of the text that makes up this section of the New Testament. This shows us that the official leaders did not have any sort of monopoly on offering wisdom and guidance.

The second indication of decentralized leadership is found in the epistles' recipients. Salutations do not indicate that the letters were intended for readers with formal and permanent leadership positions. Most letters contain no indication that they were sent from one leader to another intended as advice about how to rule the flock. To the contrary, the letters often end with long lists of salutations that strongly suggest that they were intended for public reading. In some cases they are addressed to individuals, but these were the exceptions. Most letters were an inclusive and open form of communication, which were addressed to the whole community in a location.

We need not read between the lines to find support for equality, which is directly encouraged by several passages. For example, Paul told the Galatians, "So you are all children of God through faith in Christ Jesus. And all who have been united with Christ in baptism have been made like him. There is no longer Jew or Gentile, slave or free, male or female" (Gal 3:26–28).

It is clear that all believers were to be valued equally, but the equality did not usually involve a disruption of worldly social roles. A believer might be a merchant or slave, but when they gathered they were all brothers and sisters in Christ. Their spiritual equality was in spite of their worldly inequality.

James's letter included a warning not to favor the wealthy: "Yes indeed, it is good when you truly obey our Lord's royal command found in the Scriptures: 'Love your neighbor as yourself.' But if you pay special attention to the rich, you are committing a sin, for you are guilty of breaking that law" (Jas 2:8–9).

Paul's words to Timothy might indicate a different approach, since they describe how some people enjoy a higher status than others: "In a wealthy home some utensils are made of gold and silver and some are made of wood and clay. The expensive utensils are used for special occasions, and the cheap ones are for everyday use. If you keep yourself pure, you will be a utensil God can use for his purpose. Your life will be clean, and you will be ready for the Master to use you for every good work" (2 Tim 2:20–21).

When we look closely at this passage, we find an inversion of status. The fine vase may sit in the cabinet for months while the more humble teapot is used daily, so worldly status has an inverse relationship with utility. We should also notice that the passage does not give different instructions for the fancy or plain.

On the other hand, the book of Hebrews makes clear that there is some sort of leadership that can issue instructions: "Obey your spiritual leaders and do what they say" (Heb 13:17). The plural use of "leaders" must be noted, but this still indicates that someone should be in charge.

Proper translation is essential here, as the word chosen does not support having leaders who are above question. The original Greek indicates that submission is to happen after a struggle and persuasion; we are once again guided toward a participatory style in which leaders can be challenged.[2] However, leaders do have an important role to play when

2. Hal Miller observes, "If you examine the use of *hupakouo*, which is the Greek equivalent of 'obey,' you will find that we ought to obey God, the gospel (Rom 10:16), and the teachings of the apostles (Phil 2:12; 2 Thes 3:14). Children are to obey their parents and servants their masters (Eph 6:1, 5). But are believers to obey church leaders? If they are, the NT writers studiously avoided saying so." Hebrews 13:17 uses *"peitho,* which means 'persuade.'" In a form that means "to allow oneself to be persuaded or convinced." He also notes that the second verb in the sentence is *hupeitko,* which "connotes not a

agreement can't be reached; the congregation should follow their leaders' wisdom.

Even without digging into the intricacies of translation, there is nothing in this passage that grants leaders a permanent role with any powers beyond persuasion. Our dominant paradigm attaches command to leadership, but having commanders is the way of the world that Jesus clearly warned us to avoid.

We might be confused by Paul's comments to the gathering at Corinth. In his first letter, Paul asks the Corinthians to treat him as their spiritual father (1 Cor 4:15) despite Jesus's clear warning to avoid such things. Even though he puts himself in a position of authority, he still writes: "So I ask you to follow my example and do as I do" (1 Cor 4:16). This request for cooperation muddles his supposedly paternal role, especially when we remember that he had addressed his readers as brothers and sisters a few verses earlier (1 Cor 4:6).

The case for command is further weakened by Paul's next letter to the Corinthians. He mentions that he had avoided visiting Corinth because he had a rebuke for them, but "that does not mean we want to tell you exactly how to put your faith into practice. We want to work together with you so you will be full of joy as you stand firm in your faith" (2 Cor 1:23–24). It seems that he wanted to avoid playing the boss.

Paul often shared insights about right and wrong, but when it came to prescribing action, he used words like "encourage" and "suggest" (2 Cor 8:6–10) and once wrote: "Now I, Paul, plead with you. I plead with all the gentleness and kindness that Christ would use" (2 Cor 10:1).

Another claim of authority was also tempered by context. Paul wrote, "We are not going too far when we claim authority, for we were the first to travel all the way to you with the Good News of Christ" (2 Cor 10:14). Yet he begins the next chapter as follows: "I hope you will be patient with me as I keep on talking like a fool. Please bear with me" (2 Cor 11:1). This was no way to establish an unchallenged hold on power.

Paul did occasionally use words like "command," but this was usually relaying a command from God and was clearly distinguished from his own advice (1 Cor 7:10–12). There are instances in which commands were given to Thessalonica (2 Thess 3:4–12) and to Timothy (1 Tim

---

structure to which one submits, but a battle after which one yields. The image is one of a serious discussion, and interchange after which one party gives way" (Miller, "As He Doth Serve," 74–79).

5:21, 2 Tim 2:14). But these are exceptional, and their origin is a matter of debate among scholars.[3] We may still take these at face value, which provides some grounds for giving a leader the authority to issue orders. Even so, these instances do not suggest a permanent leadership role with control over the lives of others.

Peter is often regarded as the first pope, but he also left us little to justify a rigid hierarchy. A letter attributed to him tells younger men to accept the authority of their elders (1 Pet 5:5), but this can be taken in a variety of ways; in the overall context of providing guidance without control, we should interpret it as meaning that we should follow the examples of those with more experience. To suggest that this means that older people should rule younger people is contrary to Jesus's teachings and most of what we find in the epistles.

Indeed, Peter advised elders to "care for the flock of God entrusted to you. Watch over it willingly, not grudgingly—not for what you will get out of it, but because you are eager to serve God. Don't lord it over the people assigned to your care, but lead them by your good example" (1 Pet 5:2–3).

We can find a specific example of how leadership worked in Paul's letter to Philippi. A serious disagreement between two women had divided the church, but Paul begins by addressing them directly before turning to another member: "Please, because you belong to the Lord, settle your disagreement. And I ask you, my true teammate, to help these women, for they worked hard with me in telling others the Good News" (Phil 4:2–3). He could have told their pastor to straighten them out, but instead they were viewed as peers who were responsible for finding their own resolution, even though their dispute was serious enough to concern the entire church.

## PROVING GOD'S LOVE

The charity of the first believers was not that of volunteering at a soup kitchen or donating old clothes. Sharing was a central part of the gatherings—especially the Lord's Supper itself, which was also known as the love feast.

3. Garry Wills, for example, notes that these books are widely regarded as uncertain in origin and describes them as "written in circumstances and from standpoints clearly not Paul's" (Wills, *What Paul Meant*, 16).

## ON RULES

Central authority seems to have played a secondary role in the epistles. It was sometimes called into play, but the ideal was apparently that people work things out among themselves. There were a few nonnegotiable principles like those listed by the Council of Jerusalem (Acts 15:29), but rules were not the norm.

Paul pointed toward flexibility of behavior when it came to respecting one another's values, even when it went beyond what was required by the law. He writes: "Accept Christians who are weak in faith, and don't argue with them about what they think is right or wrong. For instance, one person believes it is all right to eat anything. But another believer who has a sensitive conscience will eat only vegetables" (Rom 14:1–2).

This passage deals with food as an example, but elsewhere in the chapter he mentions other practices, and writes, "We may know that these things make no difference, but we cannot just go ahead and do them to please ourselves. We must be considerate of the doubts and fears of those who think these things are wrong" (Rom 15:1).

However, any such restrictions don't apply outside of that particular community. Paul makes this clear when he writes, "When I am with those who follow the Jewish laws, I do the same, even though I am not subject to that law, so that I can bring those to Christ. When I am with the Gentiles, who do not have the Jewish law, I fit in with them as much as I can. In this way, I gain their confidence and bring them to Christ" (1 Cor 9:20–21).

But what is to be done when a member violates the community's standards? There are conflicting messages about how to handle offensive behavior.

In Galatians Paul advises, "If another Christian is overcome by some sin, you who are godly should gently and humbly help that person back onto the right path. And be careful not to fall into the same temptation yourself" (Gal 6:1).

He counsels forgiveness in another case. "[The offender] was punished enough when most of you were united in your judgment against him. Now it is time to forgive him and comfort him. Otherwise he may become so discouraged that he won't be able to recover" (2 Cor 2:6–8). There is no mention of his being sent away, or given any specific punishment beyond the community's judgment.

This is not always the case. To Timothy, Paul strikes a different tone; he instructs that "anyone who sins should be rebuked in front of the whole church so the others will have a proper fear of God" (1 Tim 5:20).

Paul even writes to the Corinthians that a particularly serious sinner should be banished: "Then you must cast this man out of the church and into Satan's hands, so that his sinful nature will be destroyed and he himself will be saved when the Lord returns. . . . Remove this wicked person from among you so that you can stay pure" (1 Cor 5:5–7).

These examples roughly correspond to the steps of conflict resolution in Jesus's instructions in Matthew 18. I earlier noted some ambiguity about what it means to treat someone as a pagan or tax collector, and these passages together do little to clarify the matter. In the absence of clear direction, it does seem that expulsion is permissible if it is the will of the community. However, we should be careful not to claim that this is the only right way of handling serious problems.

This gives us some guidelines for internal matters, but what of external relations? It is hardly good or even possible to shut oneself off from the world. Despite our conflicting beliefs, we all must share the world somehow. Paul writes: "It isn't my responsibility to judge outsiders, but it certainly is your job to judge those inside the church who are sinning in these ways" (1 Cor 5:12). This conclusion makes clear that removing a sinner is meant to deal with believers, and not that it is a way to extend the community's values beyond its own members:

Not only should values not be imposed on outsiders, but using outside means of enforcing internal discipline is also discouraged. The next chapter shows that government should not be a tool for imposing morality within the church. "When you have something against another Christian, why do you file a lawsuit and ask a secular court to decide the matter, instead of taking it to other Christians to decide who is right?" (1 Cor 6:1)

This shows that we should not use government to impose morality, but Paul and Peter both preached obedience to government. Paul writes, "Obey the government, for God is the one who put it there. All governments have been placed in power by God. So those who refuse to obey the laws of the land are refusing to obey God" (Rom 13:1–2). He goes on to describe how good people have nothing to fear from the government. Peter echoed this, adding, "the king has sent them to punish all who do wrong and to honor those who do right" (1 Pet 2:14).

we have seen in the preceding chapters, Christianity grew out of a decentralized movement of diverse practices that were unified around Christ despite their differences. We may not be able to clearly define the boundaries where healthy diversity ended and divisive heresy began, but for purposes of discussion, we can safely say that the Way of Jesus took many paths before it became Christianity.

God's unity has never been uniform or centralized, from creation onward. God's creativity was manifested in separation—day from night, land from water, and so on. God created many types of plants and animals, whose beautiful diversity can be seen all around us. Our bodies are made of different kinds of cells and organs. Forests are made of many individual trees and other plants.

Diversity was also encouraged among humans. God changed the name of Abram to Abraham, a name that means "father of many," because he was to be "the father of many nations" (Gen 17:5). Families are divisions in humanity, and the twelve tribes of Israel were never a problem until they became competitive. The simple division of people into groups can't be the problem. Paradoxically, "united" implies multiple parts. One cannot unite, except with another.

Paul's description of how he changed his behavior when he was among different communities clearly shows us that there were diverse practices and beliefs from the beginning. Dysfunction was addressed when a practice was dysfunctional, but variation among the ecclesia was not a problem in itself. I do not claim that every approach worked well, much less that they all worked equally well. Certainly some communities worked better than others, and some practices were more widely accepted and more harmonious with what is now understood to be biblical.

The whole concept of "biblical" did not exist then. There was no New Testament in those days, with each of the four Gospels holding sway in various regions. Some ecclesias held Hebrew Scriptures to be their law, but this was contested and did not address how to live in a postmessianic age. Some people were very dogmatic about their particular ways of following Christ, but Paul was apparently not concerned with setting uniform standards, and the wording of the statement delivered by the Council of Jerusalem (Acts 15:22–31) shows that uniformity was not expected from the ecclesia.

It seems that God was content with diversity among the ecclesia. The book of Revelation is addressed to "the seven churches in the province of

Asia," (Rev 1:4) and not to seven congregations of a single church. Even in this limited region, we can see that each was clearly having its own experience and facing its own issues. Revelation's introduction continues with detailed messages to each of the churches. If God had wanted them to reunite under a single authority, this is a reasonable place to expect God to have said so. Differences were later seen as threats, and suppressed by an increasingly centralized church, but the Bible itself shows no trace of this bias toward uniformity.

When people talk about schisms in the history of the church, it is usually to refer to the splits that yielded the three most prominent divisions in the faith—Catholic, Orthodox, and Protestant. They may also mean one of several disputes over who controlled the papacy, or perhaps one of many Protestant breakups. To varying extents, these schisms have yielded large and powerful organizations with clear hierarchies not afraid to dictate to their followers. In the case of Protestant churches the body is fragmented, but the power relationships are more similar than different. Even when elected by the followers, leaders are often viewed as being above the rest of the church.

When we look at the impact on practice and organizational culture, none of these splits compares with the profound change of the often-overlooked first schism, which split leaders from followers and split the church from its original nature and Jesus's teachings on equality and power. This schism converted a decentralized spiritual movement into an instrument of empire. It was not a case of some unruly ecclesia rebelling against an established central authority; it was an attempt to use worldly power to impose uniformity among and within the communities.

I do not wish to go too far into the subject of whether and how the church went wrong since cooperation is more related to what has continued to go right around the edges of the church. Nevertheless it is important to consider how the church became as powerful as it has. To understand this change, we should look at the practices of the earliest church and compare it with what followed.

## BIRTH OF THE CHURCH

Despite the diversity among the communities in the earliest times, we may still detect some general patterns in organization. One of these was a sharing of responsibilities. The ecclesial leadership was based on the gifts of multiple members. Elders provided spiritual guidance. Deacons played an important stewardship role, administering the meals as well as the bread and wine of communion. Each part of the body had its own role to play (1 Cor 12:12–31).

It was expected that the Holy Spirit would work on the believers as a group, so there was no need for one pastor to relay the will of God. In *The Early Christians*, Eberhard Arnold wrote that, "In the first Christian communities (built with no thought of permanence and ready to break camp at any moment) the danger of disunity was overcome by the leadership in the Spirit given by the apostles, prophets and teachers, and by the brotherly love ruling among all members of the church."[1]

Tertullian was an early Christian writer from northern Africa. His *Apology* recorded of the late second-century ecclesia "that every man contributes something once a month, or whenever he wishes to, and if he can; for no one is forced, but everyone gives his share freewillingly."[2]

Outsiders were amazed by the lack of poverty, which attracted many to these rapidly growing communities. According to Arnold, "a pattern of daily life emerged that was consistent with the message that Christians proclaimed. Most astounding to the outside observer was the extent to which poverty was overcome in the vicinity of the communities, through voluntary works of love. It had nothing to do with the more or less compulsory social welfare of the State."[3]

As the generations passed, the members of the ecclesia lost their personal connections with the radical experience of the first generation of Christians. The concept of "layperson" was introduced by Clement more than sixty years after Jesus's departure. The term "clergy" did not arrive for yet another century after that, when Tertullian wrote in opposition to this divisive new concept.[4] Hierarchy crept in so slowly that this fundamental change was initially not obvious enough to raise alarm.

In 313 a single conversion had a profound impact on the course that the church would take. Ironically this conversion was sparked by a pure and simple power struggle at the end of a lengthy civil war. The man who would become Constantine was inspired by a vision to have his soldiers

1. Arnold, *Early Christians*, 38.
2. Quoted in Arnold, *Early Christians*, 117
3. Ibid., 16
4. Ibid., 237

paint Christian symbols on their shields, then routed his rival's army. He was convinced that he had won by the grace of the Christian god, and began to offer the state's favor to that god's followers. The next year he issued the Edict of Milan, which established religious neutrality for the empire and ended persecution of the believers. He later declared himself a Christian.

Once the tide turned and Christianity became associated with power, people joined the church for many reasons besides faith. Some citizens joined for political advantage or because it was fashionable. Some slaves joined because their masters converted. Within a few years, there was enough of a problem with rich men becoming clerics for tax benefits that Constantine had to legislate against it.[5]

The church grew to be more and more like government. Bishops were still elected officials, and the church was still a grassroots movement on the local level, but the beginnings of a centralized hierarchy began to emerge. The church was increasingly organized around the empire's regional centers where gatherings began to take place in formal buildings called basilicas. The government raised bishops to a rank equal to that of senator.

In 325 Constantine brought together the first comprehensive gathering of bishops, called the Council of Nicea. This was an effort to bring together diverging practices and beliefs into a single coherent religion, and was the first general assembly of the church since the Council of Jerusalem described in Acts. In order for the empire to grant favor, Christianity had to be clearly defined; a motley assortment of gatherings simply wouldn't do. Christianity was losing its coherence, and despite biblical passages that support decentralization and autonomy, those who sought a universal church needed to shore up a common base.

The Council of Nicea addressed a number of issues, but its main purpose was to deal with what was known as the Arian heresy, which held that God created Jesus from nothing. The council's deliberations resulted in the creation of the Nicene Creed, which established an understanding of the nature of God, Jesus, and the events surrounding the end of Jesus's life. The Creed addressed doctrine and not organization, but its very creation had a profound impact on Christian practice.

5. Collins and Price, *Story of Christianity*, 65

Thus they chose to live a life which stood at a critical distance
from the surrounding culture.[8]

Even today the monastic life is generally guided by adherence to a
specific set of agreements known as a rule, and this arrangement has its
origins in this period. Anthony of Egypt is credited with introducing a
practice of loose but organized lay community to these desert dwellers
during the late third century. Those who lived under his guidance shared
meals and labor, prayer and poverty.

Another desert father named Pachomius wrote what is regarded as
the first formal rule in the early fourth century. He encouraged sharing of
meals, work, and worship, and by the end of his life had established numerous communities. Three thousand followers participated in a movement that existed outside the church structure, although Pachomius's
Rule is generally regarded as the forerunner of European monasticism.

St. Basil's rule formed the foundation of Eastern Orthodox monasticism, and St. Benedict of Nursia was responsible for a dozen monasteries
that began in the sixth century, and which continue until the present day.
Basil's and Benedict's Rules were not intended as permanent restrictions;
it was assumed that as monks grew in their spiritual maturity they would
be able to provide more self-leadership. If anything, Basil's rule was intended to temper some of the zeal that was reaching dangerous levels as
hermits tried to outdo each other's asceticism with severe and sometimes
permanent health impacts.

Monks and nuns were governed by abbots and abbesses who were
elected to life terms. In some cases, membership in monastic orders grew
into the thousands, and great numbers of pilgrims added much to the
energy of this movement. The desert dwellers made immense contributions to the development of Christian thinking and practice, but the
movement did not ultimately outlive the empire that fed its growth. The
hostility of the environment was surely a reason for the movement's passing, but another cause was surely the growing division between it and the
mainstream.

Monasticism hardly died out with these first desert communities. It
just moved on to greener pastures as the Roman church itself began to
encourage lives of contemplation in settings that were much gentler than

8. Rausch, *Radical Christian Communities*, 12.

a cave in the desert. These later forms would lose many of their radical qualities and often adopted a restrictive clerical model.

The monastic impulse was absorbed back into the church, and so the last remnant of the Way submerged as the institutional path became dominant. For centuries the autonomous and egalitarian communities of the ecclesia were nearly forgotten. Christ's radical teachings and the stories of those he first inspired were trapped in a Bible that was rarely read by anyone outside the clerical elite. Grassroots communities surely continued outside papal authority, but it is hardly surprising that any historic record was lost to the Dark Ages, if it was recorded at all.

By the end of the first millennium, some established monastic orders had grown to be quite wealthy and powerful, and they perpetuated the existence of the poor by relying on serfs for labor. Wealthy benefactors sometimes meddled in the selection of abbots, with negative impacts on discipline and spiritual practices.

On the other hand, monasteries were major centers of learning, and must be credited with preserving a good deal of civilization through the early Middle Ages. Monasteries also provided relatively secure living arrangements in chaotic times, and their charity was substantial.

The shortcomings of monastic orders sometimes inspired the creation of new generations of monastic communities. For example, the Cluny movement of the ninth and tenth centuries, by putting its member communities under direct control of the Pope, sought to address some of the problems that occurred when monasteries were controlled by local political figures.

However, no reform could eliminate a natural part of the life cycle of organizations: A new organization or movement is usually inspired by some unmet need. It captures the imagination and grows rapidly. Later it gains wealth and becomes comfortable. Finally, decadence creeps in and the original energy and clarity is obscured. At such a point, ever more energy is expended by structural needs. Old organizations may linger, but the most vibrant growth must happen through the germination of new seeds.

Church history, like the rest of human history, has featured this cycle of deterioration and rebirth many times over. We now turn our attention to examples of grassroots renewal.

# six

# RENEWAL AND REBELLION

BRINGING HEAVEN BACK TO EARTH

The mustard seed is one of the best-known images that Jesus used to illustrate the kingdom of heaven. He said, "It is the smallest of all seeds, but it becomes the largest of garden plants" (Matt 13:32).

This metaphor might seem to support the growth of the church into a large organization. Indeed the church took the approach of claiming to be the only root through which truth could be drawn. However, a mustard seed does not live forever from a single stalk and crowd out all other plants in the garden. It carries within it the potential for many other mustard seeds and many generations of mustard plants, each of which adapts to the local conditions. Mustard might take over the whole garden, but only through a process of reproduction that is carried over multiple generations. A mustard seed's destiny is to make more mustard seeds.

Whatever the church's intention, Jesus was right about the mustard seed. New sprouts have popped up constantly, and no amount of weeding can stop them. These challenges have included everything from internal church reform to separatist communes to revolt. Whenever the church has neglected the cooperation that the Bible teaches, there have been people working at the margins, seeking its restoration.

To understand the renewal and rebellion that took place starting in the Dark Ages, we must briefly examine some of the ways that the Christian establishment carried out its mission. Church and state have often been mixed, so we should look at how the typical Christian commoner experienced his or her relationship to both. Much of European history has featured social and economic relationships of severe inequality and often hardship. The variation in these arrangements is beyond the scope of this book to catalog, but it is enough to say that under the feudal system most of the population lived in a state much like slavery.

The early Middle Ages, which spanned roughly the second half of the first millennium, provided much opportunity for the Roman Catholic Church to grow into a great power. The Roman Empire had collapsed, and in much of Europe there was little to take its place. This was a period of great political and economic stagnation, marked by a decline in centralized government and trade, and the loss of many skills essential to government and business function. Monasteries were almost alone in their knowledge of bookkeeping and became essential for any commercial activity. The economy had collapsed to the point that land and its produce were often the only source of wealth

Recovery from the early Middle Ages was slow, but Europe gradually began to move into the high Middle Ages. This era was marked by great variation in church organizing styles. Popes varied greatly in their character, and there were several periods during which papal succession was in dispute, but the church generally held together—although sometimes at great cost: the brutal suppression of movements that did not follow the path dictated by Rome.

During the Middle Ages, there was no landlord greater than the pope. For many peasants, the local abbot doubled as their earthly lord. In such cases, the serfs had little reason to rejoice, as the abbots who ran the ecclesial manors often did not seem particularly inspired by the Jesus' social teachings. British historian G. G. Coulton gives the rather bleak verdict that he would "judge monk slightly better than lay" in their treatment of serfs, and points to several Christian leaders of the day who argued that the monastic lords were actually worse due to the higher standards that might be expected of them.[1]

Coulton describes a grim existence in which these serfs were confronted by constant fees and forced tithing. The heaviest of these burdens was perhaps the lord's practice of taking the best animal of a deceased peasant, and the abbot's taking the second best. On the monastic manors, the abbot was also the lord and thus took both. This practice was based on the assumption that every man had cheated on his tithes during life

---

1. Coulton, *Medieval Village*, 142.

territory in such a way that allowed the foul practice. Those who harbored usurers were threatened with arrest or excommunication.

It should not be surprising that the less pious merchants sought ways to evade this crackdown; thus manuals were created to help confessors detect hidden usury through long lists of questions. Attempts at evasion continued with sufficient creativity and vigor that cases were regularly referred to Rome for guidance. Some effort went into setting a fair level of interest, but the religious thinkers of the day took a dim view of this. Florence's Archbishop Antonio threw up his hands and called the arbitrary setting of a fair price as "probability and conjecture."[8]

The breadth of the struggle against avarice was clear in Florence, which was the financial capital of fourteenth-century Europe. Even here the practice of money lending was completely banned for a time before Jewish bankers were finally brought in to conduct the dirty business of credit[9]—a flawed solution that must have played no small role in the development of anti-Semitic stereotypes. That the good Christians of Florence needed to rely on stopgap measures confirms that legal action against usury can only go so far without some sort of positive alternative.

Such alternatives were tentatively explored, and these included nonprofit facilities that offered cheap credit to the poor, along the lines of modern community-development credit unions. Parishes and other bodies also made loans, sometimes with papal approval. By 1462 the Franciscan order established lending institutions, which spread from Italy throughout the continent.

### COMMUNITY BUILDERS

The Middle Ages spawned many examples of Christians taking direct action to put biblical social values into practice. Many of these left little or no historic trace, and some were declared heretical and then crushed. Yet there are still some examples to remind us that the ways of the early believers were beginning to resurface.

One such movement came to be known as the Beguines. Their communities—called Beguinages—began to form during the twelfth century in Belgium. They originated with women who established a solitary

8. Ibid., 41.
9. Ibid., 35.

practice on the edge of towns, ministering to the poor. Often these were women whose husbands had gone off on the various crusades of that period, or who remained single because of a general shortage of men. They naturally drew together for fellowship.

By the end of the thirteenth century, most cities in the Netherlands had one or more Beguinages. There was great variation among these autonomous communities, and some limited membership to women of either high or humble classes. The largest, at Ghent, had thousands of members. Beguines maintained their own property, earned their own income, and in some cases had their own servants. They lived together in walled compounds, but functioned much more loosely than many other community movements.

An associated movement of men was known as the Beghards. These had much in common with the Beguines, although the Beghards lived communally and held their property in common. They tended to be working class, and were often affiliated with trade guilds. In some ways, they served as means of mutual aid for men who were unable to be supported by family or friends. Their mission was primarily spiritual, but they also provided significant physical support to older members.[10]

The Waldensians was another movement that embraced evangelical poverty, but which refused to submit to papal control and was therefore declared heretical. The Waldensians established communities modeled on Acts, which grew to perhaps one hundred fifty thousand members by 1500. This movement even sent out missionaries to Germany and Moravia, where like-minded ferment was underway.[11]

Other communities had a more authoritarian flavor, using the local government to enforce morality. John Calvin was the most famous leader of one such theocratic movement in Geneva, Switzerland. His followers eventually were labeled with Calvin's name. Tawney notes that for a short time at Geneva, the first Calvinists almost succeeded in their efforts "to turn the secular world into a giant monastery".[12]

Although the Genevan model involved high levels of social control, it was democratic in nature. A council of ministers elected other ministers to join them in church governance, although their choices also had

10. Gilliat-Smith, "Beguines and Beghards."

11. Holloway, *Heavens on Earth*, 27.

12. Tawney, *Religion*, 115.

to be approved by representatives of the public. The people also elected elders who joined the ministers in a leadership council called the consistory. This body did not have any formal authority, which lay with the municipal government.

Judging from the extent to which Christian values were enforced, the religious leadership seems to have had a very strong persuasive effect. Inspectors made house calls to check on the residents' moral behavior. The welfare of the sick and poor was enforced. The city was an island of sobriety and modesty, at the cost of an occasional execution or whipping.[13]

Oddly this arrangement made little headway against usurers. Tawney notes that punishing moneylenders would set a dangerous precedent. An authority of the time observed that the city was full of debtors and "if they are allowed to taste blood, who can say where their fury will end?"[14] Such fear was not baseless; as we have seen, this era was marked by many revolts in which the poor ran amok under the banner of Christ's freedom.

## THE NEW PROMISED LAND

As the industrial era began, the poor were given freedom to seek new employment, but at a cost of losing the security of the feudal manor. Caught between the strange and shifting reality of teeming cities and a decreasing amount of rural commons on which they could eke out a living, some sought to create new communities of their own. During the mid-seventeenth century, a small movement known as the Diggers created a communal arrangement by seizing private land.

Their founding document declared:

> In the beginning of Time, the great Creator Reason, made the Earth to be a Common Treasury, to preserve Beasts, Birds, Fishes, and Man, the lord that was to govern this Creation; for Man had Domination given to him, over the Beasts, Birds, and Fishes; but not one word was spoken in the beginning, That one branch of mankind should rule over another.[15]

13. Ibid., 117.
14. Ibid., 124.
15. Winstanley et al., *True Levellers*

The Diggers sought to encourage other peasants to form similar communes, concluding that there would be great resistance but that "great is the reward that will shortly be done upon Earth."[16] However, the movement never caught on beyond a scattering of imitators. In a densely populated Europe, there was not much land available for those who didn't already have it. The utopian instinct would have to move elsewhere.

Meanwhile in the Netherlands, the Labadists provided an example of how this collective relocation could occur. This movement formed under the leadership of a Jesuit-trained Frenchman named Jean de Labadie, a charismatic preacher who accumulated followers as his radical teachings repeatedly wore out his welcome with various noble sponsors. After his death, several hundred people settled in a donated castle, where they lived in community for nearly sixty years. They expanded to a number of locations in Europe and eventually beyond the continent. After an ill-fated sojourn in South America during which they discovered their general distaste for the tropical life, they sent scouts to New York, where they established Bohemia Manor.

This community adopted a rather austere lifestyle, which included complete communalism and bland food. Men and women were equal, although the community's leader seems to have had his own standards of behavior, which often conflicted with the stated values of the community. He later implemented privatization of the land, which resulted in his dying a rich man. The community collapsed within a few years and provides a warning that even the most idealistic movements are subject to problems with double standards for their leaders.

The utopian impulse also shaped many of the American colonies themselves. For example, the Pilgrims of Massachusetts reproduced the Genevan model. They viewed communalism as a temporary necessity to deal with their extreme isolation and interdependence, and dropped that approach as soon as conditions allowed. These Pilgrims sought to create a Puritan heaven in the New World but instead provoked the same sort of patchwork they left behind in Europe. Their heavy-handed theocratic approach also proved too restrictive for some, leading to the foundations of more inclusive colonies in Rhode Island and Pennsylvania, as well as a Catholic state in Maryland.

16. Ibid.

When it came time to cobble together the United States, the existence of such diverse colonies meant that it would have been very difficult to agree upon any specifics for theocratic government. In any case, the founders generally had little appetite for government-imposed morality, which was often a major reason why they had crossed the ocean in the first place.

Even after independence, the United States was a fertile ground for religious experimentation. Religion played a dynamic role in the cultural development of the nation. Huge revivals swept the land during the eighteenth and nineteenth centuries. These movements were led by flexible organizations, which were able to rapidly adapt to changing conditions.[17] Older churches, rooted and established as they were, were less able to capture the imagination of the day.[18] They were also suspicious of these revivals and their uncontrolled energy, led by poorly educated and often self-appointed preachers. Nevertheless, the people seemed to love it, and the momentum built through new sects that popped up like fresh shoots. These new believers often formed themselves into loose bodies with inclusive and democratic congregational governance.

## AMERICAN UTOPIAS

As the new American government matured, the work of building heaven on earth shifted to a loose movement of separatist communities, usually with a few dozen to a few hundred residents. These societies had names like Harmony, Jerusalem, Orderville, and even Utopia. They came out of a variety of spiritual practices but generally shared a drive to create out of raw land an ideal new society in which they would live out their particular biblical beliefs. This movement reached its peak during the nineteenth century, during which more than one hundred thousand members lived in over a hundred communities at various times.

This movement is described in great detail and with dry humor in Mark Holloway's *Heavens on Earth*, but a few highlights are worth noting: There was a tremendous variety among these communities, from ascetic to comfortable and from rigid to relatively free.

17. Collins and Price, *Story of Christianity*, 185.

18. Ibid., 190.

There were also some innovations which would generally be regarded as heretical; for example, the Oneida community practiced collective marriage, intended to overcome the supposed contradiction that people "be allowed and required to love in all directions, and yet be forbidden to express love but in one direction."[19] Another troubling development was that this community developed a high standard of living that relied on the hiring of nonmember workers. From an organizational point of view, this was a far more serious error because it involved a class of people who did not enjoy full participation in the governance of the community.

Some of these societies managed to chart a course between falling into overly strong leadership and fizzling out in disarray; one successful example was the Amana Society, which lasted for nearly a century in New York and later Iowa. There, six distinct but unified communities were established within a few miles of each other. Each village had all the amenities of a typical small town, including a school, store, shops, factories, and taverns. By 1861 they collectively worked around thirty square miles of farmland. These villages were governed by a board of trustees, which was elected annually. Women's participation in governance was limited, and the sexes were segregated from an early age. The villages also shared resources among themselves, so that the good times and hard times were shared by all the communities. Each member received an allowance to be spent as he or she chose.

This communal arrangement survived until the Great Depression, when the communities gave up their communal structure and began to encourage private enterprises. They also continued with more cooperative businesses, of which Amana Refrigeration was the most famous, although it is no longer cooperatively owned. The Amana Colonies remain a major tourist attraction, which is still owned in common.

Some groups from the Anabaptist tradition, like the Amish and Mennonites, maintain communities into the present day. The most communal of these groups is the Hutterites. In the northern Great Plains, the Pacific Northwest, and western Canada, there are still hundreds of Hutterite colonies, which practice fairly radical sharing of resources. Homes and personal possessions belong to specific families, but all real estate and everything with an economic purpose is held in common.[20]

---

19. Holloway, *Heavens on Earth*, 186.
20. Hutterian Brethren, "Organizational Structure."

the revolutionary cause. This occurred through the creation of grassroots intraparish organizations called "base communities." The movement began in Brazil during the 1960s and has since spread throughout much of the world, with concentrations in Africa, the Philippines, and South Korea.

"Base" refers to a community's role as the smallest unit of the church, usually made up of several dozen individuals who formed a community within their parish. These communities served as a forum for Bible study that was centered on members' experience as poor people, and provided a structure through which members could improve their lives in whatever way they felt collectively called.

Some of these communities were certainly influenced by the rebellions that have punctuated Latin America's modern history. Christian teachings also provided substantial inspiration to many communist agitators, but it is not fair to brand the whole of liberation theology as a Marxist cooptation of the faith. It is true that base communities sometimes took political action, but more often they simply engaged in biblically-inspired cooperation. They sought to revitalize the church from within and were building a new world within the old.

Communism was in the mix, but we should not ignore the perspective of well-informed observers like Margaret Hebblethwaite, who explains that these base communities were primarily a response to a church with insufficient pastoral resources, and that they generally took pains to remain in harmony with the Roman Catholic establishment. Indeed liberation theology stems directly from Roman Catholic social thought, first articulated by Pope Leo XIII in his 1891 encyclical *Rerum Novarum*.

Leo wrote to refute the false teachings of revolution, yet Hebblethwaite describes this teaching as an ally of liberation theology, "for defending human rights, upholding the rights of the workers, (and) insisting on the responsibilities of the rich nations to establish fairer trading relations"[24]

## PROACTIVE COOPERATION

Marx knew that communism must ultimately wait for the failure of capitalism, and that conditions have to get bad before they get better. In

24. Hebblethwaite, *Base Communities*, 166. See also John XXIII's *Pacem in Terris*, Paul VI's *Populorum Progressio*, and John Paul II's *Laborem Exercens* and *Sollicitudo Rei Socialis*.

contrast, cooperation provides a way to avoid such deterioration, both economic and spiritual. A society may be wealthy and comfortable but still lacking in justice and goodness, and Christian cooperation must go beyond mere equality of wealth. In 1961 Pope John XXIII encouraged the empowerment that cooperation provides.

> Justice is to be observed not only in the distribution of wealth, but also in regard to the conditions in which men are engaged in producing this wealth. Every man has, of his very nature, a need to express himself in his work and thereby to perfect his own being. Consequently, if the whole structure and organization of an economic system is such as to compromise human dignity, to lessen a man's sense of responsibility or rob him of opportunity for exercising personal initiative, then such a system, We maintain, is altogether unjust—no matter how much wealth it produces, or how justly and equitably such wealth is distributed.[25]

He went on to specifically note that cooperatives have a "greatness of task" that must be protected because, "by the force of their example they are helping to keep alive in their own community a true sense of responsibility, a spirit of co-operation, and the constant desire to create new and original work of outstanding merit."[26]

Pope John Paul II also noted in 1981 that capitalism and communism both fall far short of the biblical mark and reminded the church that Catholic social thought includes a long tradition of

> *proposals* for *joint ownership of the means of work,* sharing by the workers in the management and/or profits of businesses, so-called shareholding by labour, etc. Whether these various proposals can or cannot be applied concretely, it is clear that recognition of the proper position of labour and the worker in the production process demands various adaptations in the sphere of the right to ownership of the means of production.[27]

*A Christian's Handbook on Communism* also gives clear support to cooperatives and presents the faith-based Antigonish Movement of Nova Scotia as a positive example for Christians to follow. Rather than wait for the people of his region to fall under the influence of Marxist agita-

25. Pope John XXIII, *Mater et Magistra,* paragraphs 82–83.
26. Ibid., paragraph 90.
27. Pope John Paul II, *Laborem Exercens,* section 14.

tors, Rev. Moses Coady launched an educational effort that emphasized ways that the poor could help themselves out of poverty. By 1962 the movement had already birthed a cooperative factory, credit union, and other cooperative enterprises, which all helped to transform the region's economy and the people's image of themselves.

Antigonish has helped to turn Nova Scotia into one of the world's cooperative centers, and the Coady Institute continues the tradition of its namesake, training people from around the world to lead community-based development efforts.[28]

It is essential that we find ways to help develop the world's economy in more just directions, and cooperative efforts have always played a role in the struggle to bring about justice. We should take seriously the *Handbook's* anticommunist authors' recommendation that,

> Christians need to appreciate the importance of decentralization in economic life and the establishment of independent centers of economic initiatives in this day of large corporations and various state systems. They should sense what the advancement of democratic enterprises has meant to much exploited nations in Asia, Africa and Latin America.[29]

History has been marked by dramatic cycles of upheaval that are triggered by the neglect of justice. Whenever conditions are allowed to deteriorate, a response is sure to follow. This cycle will continue until we can find a path that provides the right mixture of liberty and justice.

Peasants and popes alike have recognized that cooperation can break this vicious cycle, and that it provides a valuable alternative to both capitalism and communism while offering some of the best characteristics of both. The cooperative way nurtures the free will that is obviously part of God's plan, and provides a free and orderly transition to a just society.

28. Coady International Institute, "Coady History."
29. Committee on World Literacy, *Christian's Handbook,* 76–77.

*seven*

# A NEW FELLOWSHIP

MODERN EXAMPLES OF CHRISTIAN COOPERATION

The preceding chapters have shown a wide variety of cooperative practices both written in the Bible and inspired by it. Some have worked better than others, but all can contribute to the discussion of how we should organize society. God likes diversity as long as certain principles of justice and inclusion are followed, so we have many models from which to learn.

However, one common feature of many examples given so far is that they are old. They were created to deal with conditions that are much different from those in our current era, and economic and technological changes present us with new challenges that limit their usefulness. Thus, we'll now turn our attention to models that are currently growing. These projects are the current crop of mustard plants.

Some might choose to pursue a literal and immediate reenactment of how the believers "met together constantly and shared all that they had" (Acts 4:32), but most Americans would not see such communal arrangements as an option for themselves. We might admit that this is an ideal, but we should not forget that this initial attempt at living together did not last.

The first attempt at communal Christianity may have collapsed because of the suddenness of the change. As we can see from the repeated failure of revolutions and communes, people do not move easily through complete transformation of their circumstances and behavior.

The beauty of cooperative models is that they provide an opportunity for a gradual transition to a more just world. Revolution is not necessary, and participants may become involved in building a new order to whatever extent they are ready. More models will provide more opportunities for growth and learning, and these will make it easier for us to take steps toward whatever we identify as the ultimate goal, whether that is living in common, or just buying insurance or groceries in a way that matches our ethics. Small and simple cooperatives can fit together into larger ones, providing ever more benefit to a growing membership.

Modern cooperative endeavors take many forms that resist classification. However, to help illustrate how these projects are contributing to a positive transformation that captures something of the Way, we may divide these into four categories by asking two questions.

First, how inclusive or exclusive are they?

Exclusion can take many forms, but the key question is whether membership is available only to people identified as a specific sort of believer. Motivations for exclusion may be practical, evangelical, or millenarian (i.e., having to do with the end of time and Jesus's return). Exclusion ultimately plays out as the effort of a separate people.

Inclusion, on the other hand, means that membership is open regardless of faith. This often stems from a simple desire to love all neighbors but might also be motivated by evangelism, because it provides an opportunity to bring people in without first converting them. The chance to participate in an economy based on Jesus's teachings could make someone interested in learning more about the teacher and could provide the proof of love that Jesus and Paul mentioned.

Second, does a cooperative effort provide a limited service, or does it act as a comprehensive community that meets most or all of members' daily needs?

At one end of the range, service cooperatives merely provide a service that might be used only rarely, as is the case with insurance. Others provide services that are used regularly, but even though there are frequent interactions with the co-op, the relationship among most members is much like that which a customer has to other customers at their neighborhood grocery store. Such projects are limited in their immediate capacity to transform lives, but they can serve as building blocks. More important, they provide a way for any person to get involved even if they aren't interested in communal living. Because they involve only part of a member's life, the member may join several cooperatives while their primary faith-identity remains with their congregation and their personal savings remain their own.

At the other end of this range are cooperative efforts that serve as a comprehensive communal system that meets all needs of its members, much like what is described in the book of Acts. At their best, these provide a glimpse of what it might look like "on earth as it is in Heaven." These arrangements are also quite varied. Some involve full sharing of wealth, or at least an agreement to share anything over a certain level. In others, each individual or family maintains their own finances in a way that is similar to life in a capitalist economy, but different in that most of their daily business transactions occur within the cooperative system.

There are many great examples of Christian cooperation, and what follows is by no means a comprehensive account. These groups provide a rough representation of different approaches. I have chosen projects that can easily be found on the Internet for those who wish to do further research. Links to these and other examples can be found at the Web site www.bookofacts.info.

These two sets of characteristics—exclusive and inclusive, services and systems—can be combined to create four categories. Within each are countless ways to work out our faith together, but let us look at a sampling of each so that we can understand their general characteristics.

## EXCLUSIVE SERVICES

Medi-Share and Christian Healthcare Ministries (CHM, formerly the Christian Brotherhood Newsletter) are two cooperative health-care systems. Between them, they have helped their members pay a total of $750 million in medical expenses through voluntary mutual aid. Both ministries require members to be Christians who live biblical lifestyles, which includes restrictions on adultery and drug abuse.

Both Medi-Share and CHM have multiple levels of membership, which have some similarities to different levels of insurance coverage, but for much less than what insurance costs. CHM also has a service through which members may list medical expenses that do not meet the program's guidelines, so that their fellow members can direct their prayers and make direct contributions.[1]

Medi-Share's fifty thousand members also have democratic control over their program. Its Web site proclaims that members "can vote to expand what medical needs will be shared, change member responsibilities, and otherwise modify the program. This is one important reason why our members are so satisfied with Medi-Share—they have a voice!"[2]

Amish and Mennonite farmers in Ohio have continued their traditional cooperative practices to the present day with Green Field Farms. This co-op of dairy farmers is now engaged in a major partnership with the secular cooperative that makes Organic Valley dairy products. This arrangement helps Green Field to market members' products and increase their income while still allowing them to maintain their cultural and religious integrity.

In addition to requiring sustainable and humane practices, the membership guidelines state that Green Field members must also be members of the Plain Community, and also use horse and buggy as primary source of transportation. Their guiding principles also include caring for others: "We respect all peoples within and outside of our community. We believe it is always best to seek ways to improve not just the Amish community, but the community at large."[3]

## INCLUSIVE SERVICES

Goodville Mutual was started by Mennonites in 1926 to provide themselves with auto insurance, but offers membership to the general public. It is based on Mennonite values, and current decisions are "guided by biblical principles of love, justice and integrity." Goodville has spread to nine states and now also insures homes, farms, businesses, and churches. Despite its success, it still makes a point of only working with independent local brokers. Profits are invested back into the company to benefit its members.[4]

---

1. Christian Healthcare Ministries, "How it works."
2. Medi-Share, "Frequently Asked Questions"
3. Green Field Farms, "Certification Guidelines."
4. Goodville Mutual, "History of the Company."

A Catholic lay leader named Robert Waldrop founded the Oklahoma Food Co-op in 2003 as a way to connect farmers with urban consumers. He had made personal connections with farmers while buying supplies for a Catholic Worker community but realized that direct purchasing was not convenient enough for most people. In order to help others get access to fresh local food, he organized a group to order together.[5] Their food co-op now runs a Web site that includes an e-commerce platform for sales of Oklahoma-made products of all sorts. More than one thousand consumers and one hundred producers are members of this innovative co-op. Once a month, orders are compiled and shipped around the state using a network of volunteers.[6]

Another food-related ministry is the Community Food Co-op of Utah. This grew out of SHARE, which is a nationwide food-distribution ministry that provides a monthly box of food staples to members. The Utah chapter is the only SHARE chapter that calls itself a cooperative, but all chapters use cooperative strength in numbers to help members get affordable food. The co-op is not a charity program, and the benefit to members is based on bulk purchasing. The Utah co-op now has teams at more than two dozen locations—mostly Christian churches—across the greater Salt Lake City metropolitan area. They describe their goals as reducing hunger and building community for members of all religions.[7]

EXCLUSIVE SYSTEMS

Christians living in community has been a common theme through the ages, and even our individualistic age is no exception. There are far too many such communities for this book to address them all, so I will focus on a few examples that illustrate unusual characteristics.

The first set of examples is part of a movement called "new monasticism." This loose and growing network includes dozens of communities around the country. The "monastic" label may evoke images of robes and chanting, but these communities look much like any modern group household. They are regular folks who are deeply inspired by Christ's example. They see community as a means of seeking conversion as a lifelong

5. Heffern, "Local Food."
6. Oklahoma Food Co-op, "Join."
7. Community Food Co-op of Utah, "Find a Co-op Team."

experience. This personal unfolding is mirrored in how the movement sees itself—as a decentralized effort to live by the example of Jesus.

A loose identity is formed around a dozen "marks." These are principles that are generally agreed to be indicative of their collective efforts, rather than a monastic rule in the traditional sense. These marks are distinctly countercultural, beginning with relocation to impoverished and struggling communities, which are called "the abandoned places of Empire." Here members from a variety of backgrounds connect with something like the desert experience of the early Christian hermits. Other marks include the sharing of economic resources and "conflict resolution within communities along the lines of Matthew 18."[8]

One of this emerging movement's scribes is Jonathan Wilson-Hartgrove. He contrasts the depth of faith that these communities can build with the superficial and temporary changes that often result from the more familiar form of conversion found in the altar call. "Unfortunately, we who have learned to profess Christianity in this [latter] way appear no more like Christ in actual practice than anyone else in America."[9] New monasticism seeks to help members develop a more authentically Christlike practice.

New monasticism's members often come from evangelical or Mennonite backgrounds, but they also include Catholics and Anglicans and mainline Protestants. People of many backgrounds—who supposedly can't make it through a Sunday morning together—live in intense round-the-clock fellowship in communities that have lasted as long as two decades. Doctrinal issues do come up, but the focus is kept on the practice of living together and loving one another.

New monasticism is hosting an ongoing series of "Schools for Conversion," gatherings hosted by established communities like the Church of the Sojourners, which is an established community in San Francisco's Mission District. The church is made up of thirty-five people sharing four large houses, with each household functioning as a family within the larger family.

The new-monastic network also includes the Church of the Servant King, whose members share several houses in Eugene, Oregon, where they have lived for twenty years. They operate a coffee house and commu-

---

8  New Monasticism, "12 Marks."

9. Stock, *Inhabiting the Church*, 27.

nity gathering space. This community also has a close relationship with the publisher of this book, with overlapping memberships.[10]

The Catholic Worker is an older movement with a similar emphasis on community and hospitality. It was started during the Great Depression by Dorothy Day and Peter Maurin, and now includes nearly two hundred houses and farms throughout the United States and beyond. Some are strictly Catholic, but there are also ecumenical communities. Hospitality is a major focus, and at times the members of a community may be outnumbered by guests.

In many cases, the members live together as roommates in a common house, but in St. Louis, a recent project called Dorothy Day Cohousing sought to provide more privacy for its members. They were using a cooperative model known as cohousing, in which families had their own private homes—in this case apartments.[11] Cohousing is not unique to the Catholic Workers, and other faith-based cohousing communities include Temescal Commons in the San Francisco Bay area, and Bartimaeus Cohousing near Seattle.[12]

Living in common may also include working in common. Jesus People USA (JPUSA) is an independent community that started in 1972. This community is made up of five hundred residents living in a single apartment building in Chicago, with a larger nonresident congregation. They grew out of the Jesus People—a movement of Christian hippies who set up numerous communal houses during the countercultural flowering of the 1960s and 1970s.

JPUSA now owns several enterprises, and their common work includes T-shirt printing, selling roofing supplies and siding, and working with sheet metal. Together these projects provide 90 percent of the community's collective income. The enterprises are seen as an integral part of the community's ministry, in which they can interact with the public while serving as a role model directly inspired by Acts.[13]

The community is very aware of the pitfalls of power, and to avoid those, they have decentralized their leadership. They do give authority to some leaders, but it is tempered by a desire to share power. Their ex-

---

10. Byassee, "New Monastics."

11. Doyle, "Breaking Dumpstered Bread Together."

12. Bartimaeus Cohousing at Meadow Wood. Online: http://www.bartcommunity.org.

13. See the link on the JPUSA Web site at http://www.jpusa.org/meet.html

planation of this delves into key biblical issues of leadership and divine guidance:

> The role of leadership in a community is not without difficulty. By nature, it is our inclination to desire such a role for all the wrong reasons; for honor, for prestige, for the adoration of others, or simply to prove that we are someone. In recognition of these natural tendencies that occur in all of us, we don't operate on a one-leader basis. . . . Such plurality in leadership is based on a mutual submission which can hear God's voice through the youngest community member as well as those who hold authority positions. Every healthy community has good leadership with mutual submission simply as a by-product of Christian commitment one to another.[14]

### INCLUSIVE SYSTEMS

Some systems have Christian values at their core, but are not particularly religious organizations in their daily operations. These have often started as small clusters of cooperatives and grown over the years into regional systems that welcome all their neighbors to participate. There are several such cooperative systems in Italy and elsewhere, which provide many services while keeping a loose structure that is much like the usual relationship that consumers have with the businesses they patronize. The largest such models are located in Italy and Spain.

The Confederazione Cooperative Italiane was founded in 1919 as a federation of already- existing Catholic cooperatives. It is now the largest such federation in Italy, doing nearly 40 billion euros in business per year. It has three million memberships (although some individuals may be a member of more than one co-op) and four hundred thousand employees. The federation's cooperatives are heavily involved in industries ranging from tourism to health care to fisheries and farming, and its credit unions account for more than a tenth of the Italian financial industry.[15]

The Federazione Trentina della Cooperazione was founded in 1895 and has a tight regional focus in the autonomous Italian province of Trento. Nearly half the province's population holds a membership in at least one of more than five hundred cooperatives. The federation's focus

14. Jesus People USA, "Frequently Asked Questions."

15. Confederazione Cooperativa Italiane, "Global Figures."

is in agriculture (particularly wine and cheeses) and retail (providing the only grocery store in more than two hundred villages), but there are also worker-owned cooperatives in everything from tourism to social services. More than thirteen thousand people are employed by the Trentina cooperatives, which have collective assets of more than two billion euros.[16]

The Mondragon Cooperatives in the Basque country of Spain had their genesis in a young Catholic priest named José María Arizmendiarrieta. Father Arizmendi, as he was known, was sent to this impoverished region during the aftermath of the Spanish Civil War and World War II. There he ministered to the oppressed population by founding a trade school. The school's first graduates organized a cooperative in 1956 and put their skills to work making household appliances.

The Basque cooperative movement grew by investing heavily in creating more cooperatives. Individual workers retained a capital account that they were able to cash out when they retired; until that time, the money was available for investment in new cooperatives.

Mondragon's first members were not content to improve only their own situation, and resolved to use a portion of their profits to help their fellow Basques start cooperatives. This led to the creation of an economic powerhouse, which is the seventh-largest business group in Spain. Mondragon provide jobs for more than eighty-three thousand people through more than 150 cooperative firms, including one of Spain's largest banks and the nation's largest domestically owned chain of supermarkets. It possesses nearly thirty billion euros in assets.[17]

Of the more than one hundred co-ops created by Mondragon in the first three decades, all but three survived, despite a severe decade-long recession that gripped Spain for much of that time. The Basque country had close to one quarter of its workforce unemployed at the peak of the recession, but the cooperatives kept adding jobs. Specific jobs were sometimes eliminated, but workers were retrained and offered employment elsewhere in the system.[18] The Basques have shown that there is a way to run a profitable business at a large scale while remaining true to Christian social values.[19]

16. Organisation for Economic Cooperation and Development, "Trentino Co-operative System."

17. Mondragon, "Most Relevant Data."

18. Morrison, *We Build the Road*, 172.

19. Herrera, "Mondragon."

## SOLIDARITY AND COOPERATIVES

Cooperatives are not just for those fortunate enough to live in the world's more affluent nations. Cooperation is often driven by need, and those who can't afford to take care of their own needs on their own are more likely to look for collective solutions. In many ways the global cooperative movement is stronger in developing countries, where the need for cooperation is more apparent.

Cooperation gets to the root of the economic problems whose symptoms are the inspiration and justification for much of the world's missionary work. At worst, carelessly giving aid to people in need can further disrupt local economies and perpetuate the need—the charity has good intentions, but recipients are less likely to plant crops when free food arrives by the truckload. Donated food temporarily alleviates the symptoms of hunger, but it rarely gets at the hunger's cause, which is often partly the economic chaos that has followed the destruction of traditional local economies. Cooperatives excel at providing the independence that is key to rebuilding these local economies, and at providing them with just connections to the global economy.

Just Coffee, or Café Justo, is a cooperative that provides its members with an income far above what is usually possible for small independent farmers in the Mexican state of Chiapas—their share of the retail price has increased more than tenfold. Working together, they were able to open their own roasting and packing plant just south of the U.S. border. The raw beans are shipped to this facility at the far end of Mexico, which is operated by relatives of the members. From there, the finished product is shipped over the border and distributed. Most sales are through churches in southern Arizona.

The $20,000 loan to start Café Justo came from Frontera de Cristo, a Presbyterian border ministry. This investment has made a huge difference in the lives of members, and can be regarded as a positive and humane way to discourage illegal immigration. Members have better economic stability and feel less pressure to leave their homes and families in order to look for work in the United States. Their families have health insurance, and their home community in Chiapas has safe drinking water.[20]

20. Regan, "Roasting Revolution."

Kuapa Kokoo provides another example of how we might restore justice to the global economy. This co-op of cocoa farmers in Ghana was organized in 1993 as a response to globalization's downward pressure on cocoa prices. The co-op now brings together more than forty-five thousand farmers, who enjoy a better price and better control over their growing practices. Members have used this control to move toward more sustainable techniques that lessen the need for further aid in the future. The co-op has also opened a credit union for its members, and a portion of profits are distributed on a communitywide basis to raise everyone's quality of life. It is not a faith-based organization, but its work is clearly compatible with Christian values.[21]

Kuapa Kokoo's innovation reached a new level in 1997 when it launched Divine Chocolate. Nearly half of this international company is owned by the cooperative itself, and their large share in the joint venture provides the farmers with a much larger share of the final retail price of their goods. However, they would not have been able to get off the ground without additional help, which they received from several sources in more wealthy countries. These have included Lutheran World Relief and the United Kingdom's Christian Aid, which have provided both financing and connections to market.[22]

Divine Chocolate has also enjoyed the support of a credit cooperative called Oikocredit, which has funded dozens of other cooperatives throughout the world and provides loans regardless of faith. Oikocredit provides opportunities for socially responsible investing, giving a modest return on investment. Because its mission is to support the world's poor, all member organizations have equal power; equal power is held by wealthy investors from the global north and by small investors from one of the nations in which loans are extended.

Oikocredit now has a total capital fund of over 300 million euros, invested by hundreds of churches, dozens of banks, and support organizations with a collective membership of 27 thousand individual investors. Over their three decades in operation, Oikocredit has enjoyed a default rate below 10 percent, which shows that the program is indeed providing financial stability for recipients.[23]

21. Divine Chocolate, "Kuopa Kokoo."
22. Ibid.
23. Oikocredit, "Facts and Figures."

The United States' affluence is based on the poverty of others and grows from generations of injustice, so we have a responsibility to remedy that imbalance. Here again, cooperatives can provide a voluntary way to tackle what often seems like an impossible problem. This sort of arrangement shows an integrated way that people in more affluent parts of the world can cooperate to help our brothers and sisters worldwide.

*eight*

# COOPERATIVE PRINCIPLES

OPPORTUNITIES AND OBSTACLES TO COLLABORATION

Christian values include much to support the practice of cooperation, but that is only half the picture. We must also consider whether the ways that Christians cooperate will be compatible with the modern cooperative movement.

Christian individuals have played a substantial role in the development of this cooperative movement, and many cooperatives explicitly identify with the Christian values discussed in this book. Even so, we should not take the participation of individuals and the occasional Christian-oriented cooperative to mean that cooperative development will become a widespread technique for Christian community building, ministry, and evangelism. Nor should we assume that such development would be welcomed into the cooperative movement as a whole.

The practices described in the New Testament are ultimately far more radical than most of the practices found in modern cooperatives. These differences include the extent to which property was held in common, the extent to which economic divisions broke down, the comprehensive nature of participants' involvement, and the blurring or elimination of lines between religious and economic organizations.

Many Christians may see the value of cooperatives, but can faith-based cooperative projects be integrated into the cooperative movement? Would that even be desirable to Christians? To address these questions, let us look at the standards of the existing cooperative movement, which identifies itself with seven internationally recognized principles.

The "Statement on the Cooperative Identity" grew out of the so-called Rochdale Principles laid out in 1844 by a group of English workers whose store in Manchester is generally regarded as the first successful modern cooperative. The principles have been revised over the years, and the current list established by the International Cooperative Alliance in 1995 is summarized as follows:

1. Voluntary and open membership

2. Democratic member control

3. Member economic participation

4. Autonomy and independence

5. Education, training and information

6. Cooperation among cooperatives

7. Concern for community[1]

Most of these principles provide no serious obstacles, but three do raise concerns that should be addressed in some detail: Voluntary and open membership may raise issues of inclusion for faith-based cooperatives. Democratic member control does not necessarily match the biblical model of inclusive decision making. Finally, autonomy and independence may conflict with efforts to rebuild the ecclesia as integrated bodies.

I should disclaim that I do not speak for the cooperative movement as a whole, and my analysis should not be taken as any sort of presumed final word. I am merely looking at the issues based on my experience of the movement and offering my thoughts about what we might expect from a conversation about compatibility, which will unfold through the unpredictable reactions of many individuals and cooperatives.

## VOLUNTARY AND OPEN MEMBERSHIP

The first cooperative principle encompasses two separate concepts, and we should address each separately. Voluntary membership provides us with no trouble, but open membership is not so simple.

Voluntary participation should be a key point of compatibility between Christians and the cooperative movement. We have learned

1. International Cooperative Alliance, "Cooperative Identity."

repeatedly that government cannot enforce morality beyond the short term, and does so only at great cost. Voluntary membership should help build a sense of common cause, since it reduces the risk that cooperatives will function as a communist Trojan horse. Many socialist governments have implemented things called cooperatives, but to the extent that they are extensions of the government, these false cooperatives also violate the principle of autonomy discussed below.

The worldwide communist movement has collapsed, but its underlying motivations remain. The world is stricken with a great division between wealth and poverty, and this will only get worse as resources become increasingly scarce and humans become increasingly plentiful. The embers of revolution are smoldering in many parts of the world and may ignite at any time. Rather than ignore or suppress the very real and legitimate complaints that fuel this ferment, Christians ought to once again meet the problem head-on as Rev. Coady did in Nova Scotia. His encouragement of cooperation is a tried-and-true model that worked in the Bible and works still today.

The second half of this principle provides more of a challenge to compatibility with faith-based cooperation: Organizations that limit participation on the basis of religious identity are in conflict with open membership. The Principle describes cooperatives as "voluntary organisations, open to all persons able to use their services and willing to accept the responsibilities of membership, without gender, social, racial, political or religious discrimination."

The Bible contains a strong theme of God's people separating themselves from the world. For example, Paul writes, "Don't team up with those who are unbelievers. How can goodness be a partner with wickedness?" (2 Cor 6:14). This does not bode well for bridge building, but Jesus often went out of his way to associate with those seen as beyond help, while routinely antagonizing the most righteous Pharisees of the day. Jesus's example does not seem to support limiting our interactions to relations with the like minded.

There are already examples of inclusive Christian cooperation, described in the previous chapter. These examples show that some Christians apparently believe that loving one's neighbors is more important than keeping one's purity safe from non-Christian influences. The inclusive approach does not violate the first cooperative principle, and the cooperative movement's most highly developed models are rooted in Christian values.

Even if Christian cooperation generally maintains an exclusive character, there is still potential for agreement. Cooperatives commonly set requirements for membership where it is relevant to the co-op's function. For example, agricultural cooperatives are generally open only to producers of a specific crop. Faith might also be a valid co-op membership requirement, depending on whether the motivation is practical, evangelical or millenarian.

When the reasons are practical, there are probably grounds for some compromise on this principle. For example, the joint venture between Green Field Farms and Organic Valley is one case where membership in a particular faith community is recognized as a legitimate membership restriction by a secular cooperative. Green Field has a clear religious restriction, but Organic Valley has still chosen to recognize their cooperative nature and embrace them as fellow cooperators.[2]

Housing cooperatives might also wish to set religious restrictions for membership. If the point of a living arrangement is to help one another build discipleship as Christians, then shared faith is an integral part of membership. Here, a faith requirement could thus be defended as a valid requirement. Some Christians struggle with "backsliding" into old behaviors and may seek accountability in their community. They thus might have some similarity to a group of recovering addicts who wish to live with others who share their struggle to remain sober.

Another example of how religious criteria might come into play is found in the health-care cooperative Medi-Share, which helps members pay for other Christians' medical expenses. Its Web site notes that faith is a requirement of membership, and states: "At Medi-Share, members are challenged to live their lives according to simple, biblical Principles of health and wellness. By doing so, we strive to ensure that your share amounts aren't going to fund unbiblical, unhealthy (and expensive) lifestyles, thus reducing the amount members are required to share."[3]

Drug abuse and promiscuity do increase the risk of higher health-care costs, so in this light their exclusion could be a legitimate requirement for membership in a health-care cooperative. However, we must

2. Organic Valley, "Green Field Farms."
3. Medi-Share. "What is Medi-Share?"

also distinguish between the requirement to follow biblical teachings and the requirement to believe in them. Some non-Christians live habitually chaste and temperate lives, while not all Christians hold to their ideal behavior. In this light, Medi-share's requirement is based on faith and not behavior, so it seems incompatible with the principle of open membership.

Christians have other reasons for exclusion that are less likely to gain acceptance from the cooperative movement. For example, Jesus People USA views their presence in the wider community as a powerful evangelistic tool. They hope to create a shining example of obvious social conversion. Rather than telling people how their lives have changed as a result of their faith, they now have something to show. This may be a good thing, but it is less compatible with the principle at hand.

Exclusion related to millennial anticipation is even more incompatible with the cooperative movement. Many communal efforts, including some early American utopias, have been motivated by a desire to gather in preparation for the imminent return of Christ. It seems unlikely that the cooperative movement will have much interest in joining those with such a limited identity. This may be a moot point, however, since separatist communes have often rejected all nonbelievers (often defined as all nonmembers). In such cases, there is little reason to expect much in the way of collaboration.

There is no simple answer to the issue of exclusivity. Even inclusive faith-based cooperators may feel a stronger bond with their exclusive Christian brethren than with the secular cooperative movement. Adding to the complication, individuals within many groups of Christians may hold millenarian views. Rather than opening membership to everyone as required by the cooperative identity, or rejecting their exclusive brothers and sisters, Christians may collectively prefer to create a separate movement of something *like* cooperatives, which interacts with the cooperative movement whenever it is mutually beneficial.

## DEMOCRATIC MEMBER INVOLVEMENT

Another issue to be resolved is that of the second cooperative principle, which states, "men and women serving as elected representatives are accountable to the membership. In primary co-operatives members have equal voting rights (one member, one vote) and co-operatives at other levels are also organised in a democratic manner."

The Bible clearly encourages that power be spread among the people, but it is not clear that this is similar to the cooperative model of one member, one vote. The biblical examples of group decision making were apparently not democratic as we understand the term in American politics. Some important decisions were made by a general assembly of believers, using some sort of inclusive processes, but we must be careful not to assume that this involved tallying up votes.

The Council of Jerusalem made its decision on circumcision unanimously (Acts 15:25) even though there was clearly not a unanimous sentiment. This suggests that some method of building consensus was the standard for making decisions, which helps avoid impulsive decisions and tyranny of the majority. However, in the absence of any meeting guidelines or minutes taken for the economic decisions, we have little to guide us; the exact nature of the process is a matter of speculation.

Some cooperatives also make their decisions using consensus, so as long as Christian organizations use methods that provide equality among members, consensus by itself is unlikely to be a problem. The principle already has some flexibility in how it is applied in cooperatives, so as long as Christian cooperators practice something that provides equality in governance, there is some level of compatibility between biblical and cooperative processes.

On the other hand, the selection of leadership in the ecclesia was different than those commonly used in selecting cooperative leaders. We should remember that the first deacons were selected because they were spiritually solid, and it was ultimately the apostles who delegated their authority, with the declaration that "we will put them in charge of this business" (Acts 6:3).

There are also likely to be some striking differences between what a typical secular cooperative would expect from a meeting, and what the Bible suggests: a decision-making process in which prayer and prophecy play a significant and integrated role. The ecclesia were quite different from a modern co-op meeting. The goal of the inclusion is different in the biblical case; democracy seeks to express the will of the people, but the ecclesial process had more to do with discerning the will of God.

We must also take a serious look at the role of gender. Women are welcomed as lay leaders in most churches; and in any case, cooperative projects are somewhat separate from what is generally thought of as church. Hopefully female participation and leadership won't be a direct issue in finding common ground between churches and cooperatives.

However, many Christians believe that women should yield to men's guidance, especially to that of their husbands or a male pastor. Family is also of high importance, and cooperatives are often set up so that membership is held by a household rather than by the individual. The activities of cooperatives can have significant economic impact on families, so some may regard participation in cooperative decisions as a husband's role. In such cases, women may be pushed to the margins.

Women played prominent roles in the New Testament, following Jesus's own treatment of his female disciples. He generally disregarded taboos against speaking to women or traveling with them, and when Martha called her sister Mary to skip Jesus's teachings and join her in the kitchen, Jesus replied that her learning was more important than social expectations (Luke 10:38–42).

Some biblical passages appear to place men above women, such as Eph 5:21–24, which tells wives to submit to their husbands. However, the origin of gender hierarchy strongly suggests that it is not God's preference.

Gilbert Bilezikian presents a thorough case for gender equality in *Community 101*. He begins by observing that Adam and Eve were given their work together, when "God blessed *them* and told *them*, 'Multiply and fill the earth and subdue it. Be *masters* over the fish and birds and all the animals'" (Gen 1:28 [NLT], emphasis added).That is, both Adam and Eve are to share equally the work of reproduction and economic development, and it is not until their expulsion from Eden that God declares to Eve that Adam would be her master (Gen 3:16). God's declaration is thus seen as a description of how things would be broken, and not as an ideal to be protected. Christians generally seek to redeem the world from its fallen state, so we ought to strive for redemption here too.

Bilezikian points out that the other passages often cited as support for restrictions on women come from the pastoral letters to Timothy and Titus, which were written to address ecclesia in crisis. Bilezikian outlines what he calls the "remedial model" of ministry, which was to be used under extreme circumstances. He notes that in each case where strong leadership is prescribed there was a serious and acute problem in that community, which may have threatened its very survival.[4]

The pastoral letters provide for relatively powerful leadership, but this apparently was only meant to be temporary. Once the crisis had passed, Paul probably expected that the ecclesia would revert to the more egalitarian norms found elsewhere. Bilezikian observes that "lifting those prescriptions for church order out of the Bible, absolutizing them as if they were the only model for ministry and leadership found in the New Testament, and applying them to all churches, sick or not, is a surefire method for making them all sick.[5]

In any case, Paul's occasional restrictions on women must be weighed against several passages that indicate that women were equals who participated in ecclesial leadership. We can tell that this is the norm because of the way that their leadership roles were mentioned in passing, in contrast to the specific instructions given for the crises addressed in the pastoral letters. There was no need to justify something so obvious as the need to allow everyone to use his or her gifts. Women may not have acted as bishops or apostles, but they were certainly deacons, sponsors, and organizers, which is the type of leadership relevant to cooperative efforts.[6]

The relative equality of women and men continued for centuries, and Laura Swan's *Forgotten Desert Mothers* provides a valuable survey of female leadership in the early church. She notes that female deacons were quite common and provides many examples of women in leadership, including Olympias, who was deaconess of no less a church than Constantinople's Hagia Sophia during the fourth century.[7]

Some believe that empowerment of women is a new and dangerous digression from biblical teachings, but in fact women have played empowered roles to varying extents since the very beginning. Nevertheless in many denominations, women are still regarded as men's subordinates, and this is likely to provide an obstacle that will not be easily overcome.

The cooperative movement struggles with the same sexism found in the rest of society, and most of its leadership positions are held by

---

4. Bilezikian, *Community 101*, 103.

5. Ibid., 124.

6. Women's leadership roles are noted in Rom 16:1–3, Col 4:15, and 2 Tim 4:19.

7. Swan, *Forgotten Desert Mothers*, 120.

men—mirroring the rest of our society. Hence the injection of anything that seems like a step back from equality (such as collaboration with Christian groups that may openly hold that men are superior to women) is likely to be met with great resistance. This is entirely consistent with the principle of democracy.

## AUTONOMY AND INDEPENDENCE

The fourth cooperative principle states that co-ops "are autonomous, self-help organisations controlled by their members."[8] A Christian understanding of cooperation might be more along the lines of an organization under the guidance of the church, and controlled by God.

In any case, there was no autonomous economic body described in the Bible. Some modern examples of Christian cooperation share a biblical pattern for integration, so it may not always be possible to establish where the church ends and the cooperative begins. For example, in Jesus People USA there is no clear division between community, workplace, and ministry. The enterprises generate the resources needed to sustain JPUSA's resident members, and neither the enterprises nor the residences are distinct from the church. This is in alignment with the integration of the early church but provides an obstacle to integration with the cooperative movement.

The Church of Jesus Christ of Latter-day Saints provides another example of integration between business and church life. This faith is generally held to be distinct from Christianity, but it shares a common foundation that is quite relevant to a discussion of faith-based cooperation. Mormons provide the United States' largest examples of faith-based, community-owned enterprises, so the Mormon model of integration is a useful model to consider despite theological differences from Christianity. These businesses contribute to a foundation that funds a wide variety of charities, including Christian ones such as the Salvation Army and the Saint Vincent De Paul Center.

One church enterprise was Zion's Co-operative Mercantile Institution (ZCMI), which started as part of a cooperative movement and grew to more than a dozen large department stores. It is a household name throughout Utah and beyond, as it has been for more than a century.

8. International Cooperative Alliance, "Statement on the Cooperative Identity."

ZCMI was not primarily owned by its members, so therefore was not a true cooperative. However, it was community owned in a sense, overseen by a for-profit holding company called Deseret Management Corporation.[9]

The Mormons still own several other quasi-cooperative businesses through similar arrangements, with concentrations in agriculture and broadcasting. These are regarded as separate enterprises and often overseen by the independent church-affiliated holding company Deseret Management Corporation. These businesses' management and board members are not required to be church members. They are, however, expected to conduct their business in ways consistent with the church's values. Another distinction between the Mormon enterprises and cooperatives is that profits are used to help pay the allowances of church officials, rather than being returned to members.[10]

The Mormons are unusual in the extent to which they have pursued business development, but many other churches are involved with significant property holdings and commercial enterprises. In cases where churches have commercial interests that provide financial support to their other ministries, they may not welcome competition from more independent or interdenominational Christian cooperatives. It may well be that some of today's Christian leaders, accustomed to economic power and the perks that it brings, will be reluctant to give them up. The apostles saw economic administration as a serious distraction from their true work, but they had a much fresher view of Jesus than we do.

The biblical model is to have a single organization, and this may be possible in some cases. However, many congregations may not be ready for integrating commercial activities. Churches often have well-established power structures, and in many cases it will be very difficult to have true equality within a church; pastors and other leaders will exert great influence, both consciously and unconsciously. Even in cases where the church leadership is open to letting go of the purse strings, there will still be entrenched habits of deference that hamper the development of true equality.

While the New Testament pastoral letters each related to a crisis that demanded strong and centralized leadership, the effort to restore a more

9. Sontag Bradley, "ZCMI."

10. Brady. "Church Participation in Business."

participatory culture among Christians demands more leadership from more sources. Christian cooperators might benefit from something like Bilezikian's concept of a remedial model, and begin with autonomous cooperative bodies, even if that is not their end goal. They could set their sights on the day when these new structures had matured and strengthened enough that they could keep their integrity as part of a revived ecclesia.

In other cases, the end goal might be to remain autonomous, and there is value to both approaches.

Another challenge of working within the church is that there may be unrealistic expectations. Many churches have split over doctrinal matters that are legitimate and serious, but the opportunities for trouble in typical churches pale in comparison to those faced by a community sharing all things in common.

The first believers were unified, but we now have a history of division and separation. Christians generally lack faith that we ever *could* be so unified. Trying to work within a church would encourage a sort of perfectionism that provides constant reminders of theological issues. Cooperative efforts within a church may find themselves hamstrung by rigid and conflicting views of what that church should and shouldn't do. What we need right now is a forgiving approach that looks to the next step toward whatever we hold as ideal. Independent cooperatives could remain ecumenical and build on general agreement; they would merely need to move in the right direction.

Many opportunities exist for positive work, and whether or not individual efforts identify as cooperatives or become a part of the existing cooperative movement is of secondary importance. Biblical cooperation and the cooperative movement have many complementary characteristics. There are also differences, but these seem to be reconcilable in most cases. It appears that some degree of compatibility between ecclesia and cooperative is achievable, and I hope that my framing of the issue has provided a useful start to the conversation.

*nine*

# REBIRTH ECONOMY

COOPERATION'S ESSENTIAL ROLE IN TODAY'S WORLD

Nobody on earth is generally recognized as having an exclusive direct line to God or the privilege of telling others what God wants for them. For this reason, we need a way that people of good faith can set up systems based on the beliefs that they do share. Because of the division among denominations, cooperation is as important to the task of helping Christians get along with other Christians as it is to building bridges to the rest of the population. Cooperative economics provides an opportunity to do just this.

In a sense, we can create a sort of competition among different cooperative approaches (along the same line that many churches compete for attendance on Sunday morning) while still pulling together toward the same goal. In a cooperative environment, a variety of autonomous systems may be linked to one another to the extent that their respective memberships choose. These systems will still compete for participants and other resources—much as businesses and churches do now—but the notion of a single winner may be removed or at least diminished. Once we build trust that no one system is trying to force itself upon the others, there would be an improved chance for dialog and positive exchange.

The ecumenical membership of many faith-based cooperatives is an encouraging sign that people can set aside their theological differences in pursuit of the higher good of creating community. There will always be some who focus on the differences among us, and who do not wish to associate with those with differing beliefs. Such people will be free to organize cooperatively among themselves, however restricted their definition of themselves may be. Others will be free to use cooperation to love as many neighbors as possible.

Such cooperative competition can serve as a showcase for evangelism, even among those who don't identify as evangelical. Rather than telling the world how superior they are, these various systems will have an opportunity and an obligation to put their beliefs into practice in a way that makes that superiority obvious to the world. If one system is more closely approaching God's will, we can expect it to be blessed by internal harmony and stability, low rates of departure, and general prosperity that is not based on the exploitation of others.

Instead of waiting for the kingdom of heaven—an approach, which has so far failed to bring about much visible progress—the race will be on to build it tangibly. We shall shed new light on Jesus's proclamation that we "won't be able to say 'Here it is!' or 'It's over there!' For the Kingdom of God is among you" (Luke 17:21).

## BUILDING HEAVEN ON EARTH

Most people can grasp how a specific cooperative project might help their community, but when it comes to a real transformation of the very fabric of our society and economy, we might wonder whether and how this can be possible. What will it look like to set up a decentralized, egalitarian economic system? Pushing farther, how might we set up parallel systems based on different values so we can love our neighbors even when we disagree? Could this work, or is it a naïve dream?

Far from being a dream, it is *already* working in many parts of the world. Let us return to some of the larger and more complex examples of what Christian cooperation has created.

Recall that the Mondragon cooperative system grew from the ministry of a single priest in an oppressed and impoverished corner of Spain, which was isolated under the rule of a fascist dictatorship. The Basques might have been forgiven for losing hope, but instead they worked together to improve their situation. In a half century their cooperatives have effectively taken over many functions usually considered the work of government, including health care, social security, and education. The plight of the Basque people has also provoked a stubborn separatist movement that continues to launch occasional terrorist attacks, but

Mondragon's membership has opted for the peaceful path toward economic independence. They have created a new economic system within the free market, which controls no territory beyond the real estate that it owns. No territory has ever been conquered, no land or property has been forcibly collectivized, and no one has been killed or captured in its name. Mondragon has grown through the work of people who have freely chosen to join it.

A cooperative future can also be glimpsed in Italy, which is home to several federations that are each composed of many allied but independent cooperatives. Each co-op and each federation has grown out of the shared desire of like-minded people, whether secular or Catholic, conservative or socialist. Each federation has its strengths in certain regions, but none has an exclusive territory.

Holding the Basque and Italian examples side by side, we can see the potential. Mondragon shows us the extent to which cooperatives can transform an economy, helping people to use Christian values of sharing and justice to strengthen their community in challenging times. Italian cooperation shows that multiple systems can coexist within a national economy; people gravitate towards those who share their values while those who do not agree on all the details of life can still coexist.

We have to agree to disagree and we must tolerate practices that we believe to be wrong. This is a fact of life even when we try to force our will, but cooperatives have the potential to replace many of the government functions that have become so contentious. Because each system would function separately, we would at least be freed from the twin burdens of supporting objectionable practices with our taxes while struggling to outlaw them. These controversial functions can be entrusted to a cooperative sector that combines the voluntary nature of the private sector with the democratic control of the public sector. People on each side of a controversy could build together instead of trying to tear down those across the divide.

## IN GOD WE TRUST

There are significant value differences within American culture today, and these cannot be ignored. There are also matters of agreement.

One agreement we can nurture is that most Americans don't want to force our views on other people. We would love to convince everyone that we are right, but failing that, we generally have little interest in using outright force. We do not want the responsibility or conflict that goes along with imposing behavior based on our values on people who don't share those values. Part of American culture is the principle of "live and let live." Free will is likewise a major Christian doctrine.

The actual practice of this principle is another matter. Politics in this country is a process by which competing groups of people wrestle for control of the ship of state, with different ideas of where to take it and everyone on board. When it comes to specifics, we are more than willing to impose our values, and there are some issues about which the debate is too emotional for any consideration of compromise.

When we look carefully at the general principle, a different picture emerges. It may be true that a behavior is bad and we would be better off without it. However, the very act of placing force above faith is also quite sinful, as it attempts to overrule others' God-given free will using the very powers that Jesus rejected. Even the most totalitarian theocracies have utterly failed to impose morality for long. The more energy that is put into this type of effort, the less remains for other more productive uses of government, and the divisiveness tends reinforce itself.

The problem is that we see no option. There is one government and either it goes our way (good!) or it goes their way (bad!). We need ways to avoid the false choice of "impose or be imposed upon." This would allow us to focus on productive solutions where we have agreement, and let God work where we lack agreement.

Faith requires a certain degree of letting go. If we really believe that God is in control of everything, we should have no interest in forcibly inserting ourselves into someone else's conflict with God, who doesn't need our help. God has a whole variety of ways to let wrongdoers know their behavior is out of line. The role of those who believe that they know better is to provide a better example, and not to muscle in and interrupt whatever consequences follow from someone's action.

Coercive morality has proven itself to be exhausting and draining, and in many cases the cost of forcing others to behave according to our values outweighs the benefits. Cooperative competition can help us shift our focus from the content of the decision to the process by which it is made. This can provide reason to celebrate when decisions are made in a positive and collaborative way, more justly than before.

One example of how cooperative competition might play out could be in regard to health care. We are not likely to reach a national consensus on how to define a family or what health-care services to provide under which circumstances. The division is such that it is simply not worth trying to bridge the gap of disagreement. Instead, we ought to be putting our efforts toward building upon existing agreement on either side of the gap.

Medi-Share and Christian Healthcare Ministries already provide programs that support only biblical lifestyles, while secular health-care co-ops like Group Health or the Ithaca Health Alliance make no such restrictions. In each case, these models could all be expanded and reproduced by like-minded people in other locations. These could form federations with other cooperatives to achieve economies of scale. Our current profit-based medical system may eventually be replaced by a new kind of health coverage, which could be provided by medical facilities that are part of much larger cooperative systems. Each would be based on the needs and wishes of its respective members. And of course, people could also choose to buy insurance from for-profit companies.

The failure of our current insurance system is becoming clearer as time goes on, and we cannot afford to rely on government solutions when there is no agreement about what solutions are appropriate. We may not agree on exactly what should replace private insurance, but if we can build an understanding about how groups of people can address the problem, we'll be a lot closer to meeting people's needs.

## BLESSED ARE THE PEACEMAKERS

Cooperatives also provide a key to interfaith reconciliation. In the fall of 2007, more than a hundred Muslim leaders wrote an open letter titled "A Common Word Between Us and You"[1] to the world's Christians. A response was promptly written and eventually signed by hundreds of Christian leaders, including the president of the National Association of Evangelicals. Both letters acknowledged that Christianity and Islam are distinctly different religions but agreed that they share a common core of two great commandments—to love God and to love our neighbors. They also agreed that we have work to do on loving our neighbors, and that the stakes are high.

1. Ababakar, "Common Word."

The Christian response concludes, "We are persuaded that our next step should be for our leaders at every level to meet together and begin the earnest work of determining how God would have us fulfill the requirement that we love God and one another. It is with humility and hope that we receive your generous letter, and we commit ourselves to labor together in heart, soul, mind and strength for the objectives you so appropriately propose."[2]

Only God knows where this all will lead, but we should note that Islam has its own strong cooperative traditions. Muslims have created many of the world's largest mutual insurance companies and an extensive interest-free finance system, as well as innovative housing cooperatives.[3] We must also remember that the Old Testament teachings described in chapter 2 of this book are common to Jewish traditions. Furthermore, Judaism brought the world the communal farms known as "kibbutzim" and the less-famous and more loosely collective villages known as "moshavim," as well as a variety of other cooperatives.

Each faith has its own well-established and often incompatible forms of worship, so tangible collaboration can only go so far. However, there is already common ground around cooperative enterprises. We may not precisely agree about why God wants us to cooperate, but we know that this is the essence of God's command to love our neighbors. We might take advantage of this shared teaching of cooperation as a way to build a tangible expression of neighborly love, for the benefit of our entire pluralist civilization.

This is not mere speculation; at least one example already exists: Mirembe Kawomera is a Ugandan coffee growers' cooperative that brings together hundreds of families of all three Abrahamic faiths. Each religion is represented on the cooperative's board. Their production is severely limited by a lack of capital, but they have already accomplished much more than mere coffee production. A Web site dedicated to interreligious dialogue and peace declares, "Uganda's history of religious and tribal divides is put in the past by this cooperative's emphasis on respect and diversity."[4]

---

2. Attridge, "Loving God and Neighbor Together."

3. For more information on other traditions' cooperative activity, please visit the links page at www.bookofacts.info.

4. See www.irfwp.org/links.shtml.

Closer to home, Interfaith Business Builders is based in Cincinnati. Its members are religious organizations that seek to create healthy and empowered communities through the creation of cooperatives. They seek to pull together people of varying faiths and build relationships of trust. Their goals include job creation and building relationships in the community. Their work provides people with skills in business and also democratic organizing.[5]

A case can be made for withdrawing from our current society and only working with other believers (however they may be defined). Paul's rhetorical question about good teaming up with wickedness (2 Cor 6:14) is only one example of scriptural support for the exclusive approach.

Still, how can we justify a nice comfortable separation, hunkering down with like-minded people as the world falls apart? How can we dismiss peace-loving, God-fearing people as wicked just because they fear God differently than we do? Jesus's time in the Samaritan village suggests that their having different religious beliefs—or no religious beliefs—is not sufficient grounds for turning our backs on our neighbors. Who is more wicked? Is it someone who goes to church regularly and spends their weeks oppressing their employees, or someone who does not self-identify as a Christian but is a dedicated servant to the poor?

## BACK TO BASICS

Jesus said, "A healthy tree produces good fruit and an unhealthy tree produces bad fruit" (Matt 7:17). From this we may conclude that our current order is unhealthy. The war, hunger and poverty that our current system has spawned is certainly bad fruit, and it is difficult to find biblical justification for the immense wealth that some of us enjoy at others' expense, or the greed and envy that such wealth inspires.

Technology has created a bounty that could reduce workloads and improve quality of life worldwide, but the elite that control the technology have used it in ways that create dramatic division, alienation, fear, dishonesty, poverty, suffering, war, and disease in the name of profit. Drug abuse is rampant as coping mechanism, and community is disintegrating around us. Our fancy toys and consumption can distract us, but they cannot change the grim picture.

5. Interfaith Business Builders, "About Us."

At the same time, the abundance of cooperative models—of which the examples cited in this book is a minute fraction—prove that another world is already arriving. We have no excuse to throw up our hands and declare that our current reality of poverty and war is inevitable. That is a lie that we must clearly rebuke with more than our words. Action is required. As Jesus said, "Your love for one another will prove to the world that you are my disciples" (John 13:35).

One does not need to be Christian to sense a looming crisis, but those who take the book of Revelation literally should note the similarities between the United States' place in the world and the description of fallen Babylon: "For all the nations of the world have drunk the wine of her passionate immorality. The rulers of the world have committed adultery with her, and merchants throughout the world have grown rich as a result of her luxurious living" (Rev 18:3).

The United States' wealth is the result of centuries of injustice—from the extermination of the native population, to widespread use of slaves, to the unfair trade practices of the colonial and modern eras—and some sort of atonement for that is necessary. This could come in the form of just trade arrangements and technical assistance to the world's poor, but ultimately the scarcity of resources will demand that we find ways to make do with less.

There is no doubt that a just reconciliation will be challenging, and will bring us up against all sorts of raw edges. Real justice may be a scary thought, but God never said this all would be easy. At least the sharing that cooperatives encourage will help to lessen the sting of decreased personal consumption. This help may come through everything from local food distribution to co-ops for the sharing of expensive but rarely used household tools.

The tragic reality is that most people do not see an alternative to our current system. Discouragement is our greatest enemy, and the positive models like those outlined in this book are needed to build inspiration and hope. Cooperatives show how we can overcome our divisions without having one side eventually win the battle and force its will on the other. God made us different, and difference is a fact of our life together. We cannot expect that everyone will reach a general agreement anytime soon, so we much work around that difference.

Cooperatives are generally a pale imitation of the communalism of the first believers. They still operate within the dominant system of competition, using the same principles of scarcity that Jesus came to over-throw. They may be cooperative internally, but they are still somewhat competitive with the rest of the world, and sometimes with each other.

Still, cooperatives provide steps in the right direction, baby steps toward a better way of being together. They are both testing grounds and building blocks for the new order of freedom, equality, and justice that God demands of us. Only God knows exactly what the end result of such a collective conversion might be, but we can discern its outlines in the courageous experiments like Jesus People USA and Mondragon, Divine Chocolate and Oikocredit, credit unions and homeschooling co-ops, and intentional communities of all shapes and sizes.

Cooperatives can also slow or reverse the disintegration of community. As it is, most Christians have a gaping chasm between the economic and organizational lessons they might hear on Sunday morning and the dog-eat-dog world they face on Monday morning. The rest of the week is no better, and no midweek service will change the fact that we suffer under a system that keeps us apart, jealously eyeing each other's stuff.

True love is not possible between a person who is hungry and an-other who must warily guard her plate. Rather than continuing to preach love while participating in a system based in the fear that our neighbors will get our stuff, we must find ways to bridge this gap. Cooperatives at least interrupt the practice of fear and give us an opportunity to come together on some level, to experience a real tangible love for a change.

## TRY, TRY AGAIN

Samuel Huxford compared the incident in which Ananias and Sapphira were struck dead in Acts to the initial fall of Adam and Eve. Jesus had come to restore humanity, and the hoarding of wealth in the presence of hungry brothers and sisters was clearly not compatible with his mission. Jesus's demand that the wealthy young man give away his possessions (Mark 10:17–30) was not a fluke, but the keystone of community.

Huxford points out that "when the severe punishment that Ananias and Sapphira received is coupled with the fact that Luke [the author of Acts] never again says that there were no needy people among them nor that people were selling all their property etc., it seems reasonable to think that their story is bigger than one might first think."[6]

Indeed, this was a major turning point between a community without poverty and another—a mere chapter later—in which people are arguing over portions at the common meal (Acts 6:1). For a brief shining moment the believers had slipped out of the old, corrupted ways of being, and had eliminated poverty! We cannot overstate the tragedy of this accomplishment's being undermined by the hypocrisy of Ananias and Sapphira.

The bold experiment described in the book of Acts did not continue for long. However, the successes of many other cooperative efforts suggest that this failure was because of specific conditions that can be avoided, and that common industry would have made for more sustainable abundance.

First, the change was too abrupt; the participants did not have a chance to adjust to the freedom and responsibility that comes with equality and voluntary sharing. Add in rapid growth, language difficulties, and persecution, and you have very poor conditions for developing a sustainable new social order.

Cooperatives provide the best of old and new, and an orderly transformation to a new world. We do not have to suffer through the disruption of having our government and economy overthrown, but we can start to build a new system that better serves our needs. Cooperatives provide a way to remove competition and profit as the primary motivators for commerce without discarding our whole economic order.

The beauty of the cooperative approach is that we don't have to decide how far we are going before we set out. The transition and testing that cooperation provides is highly important because gradual shifts toward sharing of wealth have shown themselves to be more sustainable than sudden lurches. This is clear from the great and growing divide between the poor and wealthy that is now found in postrevolutionary Russia and China.

The second complication that we can see in Acts is that wealth was shared, but there were apparently no means for collective generation of wealth. It seems that most of their income was from newcomers who donated their belongings. Some believers did take time to work and make

6. Huxford, "How Communal Is Community," 23.

*conclusion*

It will be a long walk to the Promised Land, but creating cooperatives provides a first step. I hope that *Holy Cooperation!* has inspired you to take action, and that your action is fruitful. This is not a time for inspiring books that get put on the shelf and fade into memory. This is a time for action, and to help you act, I would like to conclude with some suggestions for how to organize cooperatively.

This is not an easy list of principles or a simple worksheet to fill out. There is a lot of work involved in starting something like Mondragon, or even a simple co-op to share tools.

How do you get from a vacant supermarket to a community-owned store? How do you transform blighted housing into a place the residents care for because they own it? How do you take a need that you have discerned in your community and fill it with a real and tangible cooperative?

When starting a co-op, it is very helpful to have an understanding of the big picture you hope to address. This helps participants understand the scope of the project and to develop realistic expectations about the timeline. The big picture also helps to keep the development process running smoothly. Think of this in the same way that you would paint a literal picture; you begin with the general outlines and then fill in details as you go.

Having a shared model for how to proceed will also help you bring your focus back to the tasks that are of more immediate importance. For example, it is important to establish exactly what you are trying to do with your cooperative before you put too much energy into discussing its location and layout. When discussion wanders to decisions that are further down the line, it is helpful to recall the larger process and bring your attention back to more immediate tasks.

There are a number of different models for this process, and the one described here may not necessarily be the best for you. However, it is always helpful to have guidelines to keep your group focused. That way you can better understand the importance of what you are doing at a given time, and see how it fits into the big picture. What follows will provide you with a starting point for cooperation.

This is a rough outline, based on my experience of working with co-op planning groups. These steps should help to keep your efforts on track, and help you avoid some common pitfalls.

There is an abundance of resources for cooperative development, in online resources, trainings and conferences, and organizations that specialize in cooperative business advising. Links to some of these resources can be found at http://www.bookofacts.info, or by doing a Web search for "cooperative development" or "cooperatives."

The following outline will provide a basic understanding of the road ahead, and a list of questions to discuss with each step. These steps are a broad overview, and you will be most likely to succeed if you have some sort of specialized help. The more you know, the better.

## DISCERNING THE VISION

Cooperatives by their very nature are dependent on the visions and views of their members, so it is impossible to predict what form or direction they will take. It is important to clarify your assorted personal visions into a single collective vision, so you will want to answer the following questions:

- What is the need to be met?
- How could you meet this need?
- What are your organizational options? Is a cooperative the best model?
- Who are the interested parties (sometimes called stakeholders)?
- Who are potential collaborators?
- What is the business environment?
- Do you want to be inclusive or exclusive?

Once you have the outlines of what you are trying to create, you may also wish to do a web search to see if there are any models out there (i.e., "carpet cooperative" or "boat co-op"). The Web site at www.bookofacts.info has a growing list of faith-based cooperatives, and even if you are not interested in working with secular co-ops, they can still provide you with valuable examples of what works and how.

If you are really inspired and want to create your own Mondragon, have patience. The world's great cooperative systems all started as a single co-op. You'll need to focus on getting your first project off the ground before you start trying to juggle several. Even though you probably shouldn't try to start a bunch of co-ops at once, you can lay the groundwork by deciding from the start that a portion of your profits will go towards developing more cooperatives. This adds another layer of complexity to creating a shared vision, but it is helpful to develop this sort of understanding early on.

Any co-op planning group is likely to encounter differing visions, and it is always wise to get a clear understanding of the collective goals early in the process. If you can clearly agree about what you are setting out to do, your group will enjoy better focus and be less likely to experience a division based on misunderstanding your goals. Please try to avoid making assumptions about what other people in your group believe about the project.

## GETTING ORGANIZED

Once you have identified the need to be met by your cooperative, a good structure will provide you the foundation for your ongoing work together. Here are some organizational questions to ask yourselves:

- How are decisions made, communicated, and recorded?
- Who makes what sorts of decisions?
- What committees and roles will you need?
- What responsibilities and decisions will be delegated, and to whom?
- What legal form will your cooperative take?

There are a great many resources about consensus decision making online and elsewhere. I highly recommend that you do some research on meeting process. Also, always take clear notes at meetings, highlighting decisions and commitments for future reference.

## REALITY CHECK

If it is going to be independent of your church, your cooperative needs to be a sustainable business. Therefore, you need to determine if your cooperative is likely to work out financially. This process usually involves hiring an outside expert to conduct a feasibility study, which will determine whether your proposed business is likely to succeed in your market. This study can be very expensive, but it is quite important. You could lose much larger amounts of money in a business failure, and that would make loving each other more challenging than it needs to be.

A feasibility study will address:

- What are the demographics for the area?
- What competition will you face?
- How much will it cost to open the business?
- What sort of cash flow is projected?
- What sites are available and suitable, at what cost?

The results of your feasibility study will help you decide whether to move forward. In the event of marginal feasibility, you may need to redesign the project.

## BUILDING YOUR MEMBERSHIP

While you have already developed an informal membership, this is the point at which you start aggressively seeking additional members and other funding to help capitalize the business. This step involves the conversion of your feasibility study into a business plan, which shows that you know how you will achieve those feasible results. Many people will want to see a business plan before they contribute their time or money. Here are some guiding questions for drafting a business plan:

- How many members are to be recruited? How much equity is to be raised?

- Is the definition of membership clearly decided and presented? This should include share prices, payment options, member rights and responsibilities, classes of stock, and revocation or sale.

- How will you keep track of member contributions? This is extremely important.

- How will you raise funds through member loans or donations?

You will need to raise a substantial portion of your funds from members—probably close to half. However, once you have secured member equity and other funds, you might need to borrow additional money. A solid business plan will be essential. Many banks are unfamiliar with cooperatives, but having a clear business plan will strengthen your case. Credit unions often cannot give business loans but may be able to point you in the direction of a sympathetic banker.

## SOWING THE SEED

Once you have your financing lined up, you make a final decision whether to move forward. This is a very long, complicated, and expensive step. So you should seek expert guidance as much as possible. You should answer the following questions before you enter the startup phase:

- What qualifications are needed for management? Who are your candidates?

- Do you want a separate project manager to oversee the opening process?

- What facilities and equipment are needed? How will you carry out necessary renovations?

- How will you handle accounting and control functions?

- What are your operating policies?

- When do you hope to open? This can happen in stages, but should be well thought out.

It will often take a year or two to get to the point of opening the doors, and you may have to change your target date.

Starting any business takes careful planning, and cooperatives have an additional cat-herding aspect that solitary entrepreneurs don't face. Be prepared for a long and challenging road, but be encouraged; you have lots of company. Please keep in touch through the online forum at www.bookofacts.info, or by sending an email to me at info@bookofacts.info. I'll send out occasional updates as more resources become available.

I now turn this over to you. You are the ones who know what God is doing in your neighborhood, and how cooperation should be applied. You have the resources and knowledge to build whatever you feel called to build. You have a seed in your hands. Where will you plant it?

# bibliography

Ababakar, Muhammadu Sa'ad, et al. "A Common Word Between Us and You." Online: www.acommonword.com.

Alexander, David, and Pat Alexander, editors. *Zondervan Handbook to the Bible.* 3rd edition. Grand Rapids: Zondervan, 1999.

Amana Colonies. "The Amana Colonies Story." Online: http://www.amanacolonies.org/history.htm.

Arnold, Eberhard, editor. *The Early Christians in Their Own Words.* Translated and edited by the Society of Brothers. Farmington, PA: Plough, 1970.

Atkerson, Steve, editor. *Toward a House Church Theology.* Atlanta: New Testament Restoration Foundation, 1996.

Attridge, Harold W., et al. "Loving God and Neighbor Together: A Christian Response to 'A Common Word Between Us and You.'" Online: www.yale.edu/faith/about/abou-commonword.htm.

Baranowski, Arthur R., in collaboration with Kathleen M. O'Reilly and Carrie M. Piro. *Creating Small Faith Communities: A Plan for Restructuring the Parish and Renewing Catholic Life.* Cincinnati: St. Anthony Messenger, 1988.

Bell, Rob. *Velvet Elvis: Repainting the Christian Faith.* Grand Rapids: Zondervan, 2005.

Berryman, Phillip. *Liberation Theology: The Essential Facts about the Revolutionary Movement in Latin America—and Beyond.* New York: Pantheon, 1987.

Bilezikian, Gilbert G. *Community 101: Reclaiming the Church as a Community of Oneness.* Grand Rapids: Zondervan, 1997.

Bonhoeffer, Dietrich. *Life Together.* Translated, and with an introduction by John W. Doberstein. New York: Harper, 1954.

Brady, Rodney H. "Church Participation in Business." *About Mormons.* Online: http://www.lightplanet.com/mormons/daily/business/Church_EOM.htm.

Brewin, Kester. *Signs of Emergence: A Vision for the Church That Is Organic/Networked/Decentralized/Bottom-Up/Communal/Flexible/Always Evolving.* Grand Rapids: Baker, 2007.

Byassee, Jason. "The New Monastics." *Christian Century,* October 15, 2005. Online: http://www.christiancentury.org/article.lasso?id=1399.

Chadwick, Owen. *A History of Christianity.* New York: St. Martin's, 1996.

Christian Healthcare Ministries. "How it works/How To Join." Online: http://www.cbnews.org/howitworks.asp.

Church of the Sojourners. "Who We Are." Online: http://www.churchofthesojourners.org/who.

Claiborne, Shane. *The Irresistible Revolution: Living as an Ordinary Radical.* Grand Rapids: Zondervan, 2006.

Coady International Institute. "Coady History." Online: http://www.coady.stfx.ca/history.cfm.

Collins, Michael, and Matthew A. Price. *The Story of Christianity: A Celebration of 2000 Years of Faith.* New York: DK Publishing, 1999.

Committee on World Literacy and Christian Literature. *A Christian's Handbook on Communism.* 3d edition. New York: National Council of the Churches of Christ in the U.S.A. Office of Publication and Distribution, 1962.

Community Food Co-op of Utah. "Food Co-op Basics: Our Mission." Online: http://www.crossroads-u-c.org/cfc/the_basics/our_values.html.

————. "The Community: Find a Team." Online: http://www.crossroads-u-c.org/cfc/the_community/find_coop_team.html.

Confederazione Cooperative Italiane. "Global figures (December 31, 2003)." Online: http://www.confcooperative.it/C6/Global%20Figures/default.aspx

Coulton, G. G. *The Medieval Village.* New York: Dover, 1989.

Dalton, George, editor. *Tribal and Peasant Economics: Readings in Economic Anthropology.* American Museum Sourcebooks in Anthropology. Garden City, NY: The Natural History Press, 1967.

Denlinger, A. Martha. *Real People: Amish and Mennonites in Lancaster County, Pennsylvania.* 3d edition. Scottdale, PA: Herald, 1984.

Deseret Management Corporation. "Mission Statement." Online: http://www.deseretmanagement.com/?nid=3

Desjardins. "Desjardins figures." Online: http://www.desjardins.com/en/a_propos/profil/difference/chiffres.jsp

Divine Chocolate. "Kuapa Kokoo." Online: http://www.divinechocolate.com/about/kokoo.aspx

Doyle, Amanda E. "Breaking Dumpstered Bread Together." Online: http://www.thecommonspace.org/2003/01/communities.php

Ellul, Jacques. *The Subversion of Christianity.* Translated by Geoffrey W. Bromiley. Grand Rapids: Eerdmans, 1986.

Fellowship for Intentional Communities. Intentional Communities Directory. "Temescal Commons Cohousing." Online: http://directory.ic.org/records/?action=view&page=view&record_id=6221

Gilliat-Smith, Ernest. "Beguines and Beghards." Online: http://www.newadvent.org/cathen/02389c.htm

Goodville Mutual. "History of the Company." Online: http://www.goodville.com/aboutus/history.cfm

Green Field Farms. "Certification Guidelines (Revised July 13, 2005)." Online: http://www.gffarms.com/about.asp?section=83&page=883

Hebblethwaite, Margaret. *Base Communities: An Introduction*. London: Geoffrey Chapman, 1993.

Heffern, Rich. "Local Food." *National Catholic Reporter*, September 14, 2007. Online: http://ncronline.org/NCR_Online/archives2/2007c/091407/091407m.php

Herrera, David. "Mondragon: A For-Profit Organization That Embodies Catholic Social Thought." In "Catholic Social Thought and Management Education," Special issue, *St. John's University Review of Business* 25 (2004) 56–68. Online: http://www.stjohns.edu/media/3/998412b80a354217a89c869400427929.pdf

Holloway, Mark. *Heavens on Earth: Utopian Communities in America*. New York: Dover, 1966.

Hutterian Brethren Schmiedeleut Conference. "Organizational Structure of a Hutterian Community." Online: http://www.hutterites.org/organizationStructure.htm.

Huxford, Samuel. "How Communal is Community." Walker Lecture. European Evangelistic Society North American Christian Convention 25, June 29, 2006. Online: http://www.eesatlanta.org/files/walker/nacc25_huxford.pdf

Interfaith Business Builders. "About Us." Online: http://www.interfaithbusinessbuilders.org/about.php

International Cooperative Alliance. "Statement on the Cooperative Identity (1995)." Online: http://www.ica.coop/coop/principles.html

Jesus People USA. "Frequently Asked Questions." Online: http://www.jpusa.org/faq.html

———. "Meet Our Family." Online: http://www.jpusa.org/meet.html.

Just Coffee. "Just Coffee Mission and Goal." Online: http://www.justcoffee.org/Company__rev3.shtml

Kimball, Dan. *The Emerging Church: Vintage Christianity for New Generations*. With commentary by Rick Warren. Grand Rapids: Zondervan, 2003.

King, C. Harold. "The Origin and Spread of Christian Monasteries." In *The Rise of Christianity*, edited by Don Nardo. San Diego: Greenhaven, 1999.

Medi-Share. "Frequently Asked Questions." Online: http://medi-share.org/faq.aspx

———. "What Is Medi-Share?" Accessed April 24, 2008. Online: http://medi-share.org/what_is_medishare.aspx.

McLeod, Andrew. Book of Acts Project. Online: http://www.bookofacts.info

———. Notes from personal visit to Church of the Sojourners. February 2–4, 2007.

Miller, Hal. "As He Doth Serve." In *Toward a House Church Theology*, edited by Steve Atkerson, 74–79. Atlanta: New Testament Restoration Foundation, 1996.

Mirembe Kawomera. "The Peace Kawomera Cooperative." Online: http://www.mirembekawomera.com/cooperative.

Mondragon Cooperación Cooperativa. "Most Relevant Data (December 31, 2006)." Online: http://www.mcc.es/ing/magnitudes/cifras.html

Morrison, Roy. *We Build the Road as We Travel*. Philadelphia: New Society, 1991.

Myers, Joseph R. *Organic Community: Creating a Place Where People Naturally Connect*. Grand Rapids: Baker, 2007.

Nardo, Don, editor. *The Rise of Christianity*. Turning Points in World History. San Diego: Greenhaven, 1999.

National Cooperative Business Association. "Co-op Statistics." Online: http://ncba.coop/abcoop_stats.cfm

New Monasticism. "The 12 Marks of a New Monasticism." Online: http://www.newmonasticism.org/12marks/12marks.php

North, Gary. "Capitalism and the Bible." Online: http://www.garynorth.com/public/department57.cfm

Oikocredit. "Facts and Figures (March 31, 2008)." Online: http://www.oikocredit.org/site/en/doc.phtml?p=FFNew

Oklahoma Food Co-op. "Join the Oklahoma Food Cooperative." Online: http://www.oklahomafood.coop/okfoodservice.php.

Organic Valley. "Green Field Farms and Organic Valley/CROPP Cooperative Announce Major Partnership," press release, March 16, 2006. Online: http://wwworganicvalley.coop/newsroom/article.html?cat=1&id=234

Organisation for Economic Co-operation and Development. "Trentino Co-operative System." Online: http://www.oecd.org/dataoecd/20/23/37741957.pdf

Pagitt, Doug, and Tony Jones, editors. *An Emergent Manifesto of Hope.* Grand Rapids: Baker, 2007.

Pope John XXIII. *Mater et Magistra.* Online: http://www.vatican.va/holy_father/john_xxiii/encyclicals/documents/hf_j-xxiii_enc_15051961_mater_en.html.

———. *Pacem in Terris.* Online: http://www.vatican.va/holy_father/john_xxiii/encyclicals/documents/hf_j-xxiii_enc_11041963_pacem_en.html

Pope John Paul II. *Laborem Exercens.* Online: http://www.vatican.va/edocs/ENG0217/_INDEX.HTM

———. *Solicitudo Rei Sociales.* Online: http://www.vatican.va/edocs/ENG0223/_INDEX.HTM

Pope Paul VI. *Populorum Progressio.* Online: http://www.vatican.va/holy_father/paul_vi/encyclicals/documents/hf_p-vi_enc_26031967_populorum_en.html

Rausch, Thomas P. *Radical Christian Communities.* Collegeville, MN: Liturgical, 1990.

Regan, Margaret. "Roasting Revolution." *Tucson Weekly,* February 8, 2007. Online: www.tucsonweekly.com/gbase/Tools/PrintFriendly?url=%2Fgbase%2FMusic%2FContent%3Foid%3Doid%253A92309

Rutba House, editors. *School(s) for Conversion: 12 Marks of a New Monasticism.* Eugene, OR: Cascade, 2005.

Schaeffer, Francis A. *A Christian Manifesto.* Wheaton: Good News, 2005.

Sonntag Bradley, Martha. "ZCMI." Online: http://historytogo.utah.gov/utah_chapters/pioneers_and_cowboys/zcmi.html

Stock, Jon R., et al. *Inhabiting the Church.* Eugene, OR: Cascade, 2007.

Swan, Laura. *The Forgotten Desert Mothers: Sayings, Lives, and Stories of Early Christian Women.* New York: Paulist, 2001.

Tawney, R. H. *Religion and the Rise of Capitalism.* Glouchester: Harcourt Brace, 1926.

Tyndale House Publishers. *Holy Bible: New Living Translation.* Wheaton: Tyndale, 1996.